T0365214

"With the Master was a noted Bahá'í physician, Dr. Yunís Khán-i-Afroukhtih. 'Abdu'l-Bahá turned to him and remarked in a spiritually playful way, 'Fádil was introduced to the Faith by us; let us now see the difference between one that we have taught and one taught by yourself '. In deference, the amiable doctor humbly observed, 'Your Honour, whatever we deliver is like a copper coin, what you deliver is 'gawhar-i-shab chirágh' (a radiant gem)'." Page 66

A RADIANT GEM
A Biography of Jináb-i-Fádil-i-Shírází

A RADIANT GEM
A Biography of Jináb-i-Fádil-i-Shírází

By
Houri Faláhi-Skuce

Shaykh Muḥammad-Ibráhím
Fáḍil-i-Shírází

This book is dedicated

In loving memory of my dear mother,

Subhániyyih Fádil-Faláhí

www.trafford.com

North America & international
toll-free: 844-688-6899 (USA & Canada)
fax: 812 355 4082

Contents

Acknowledgements

I am greatly indebted to the Universal House of Justice for its assistance and guidance and for allowing its research department to make available to me copies of Tablets revealed by 'Abdu'l-Bahá for Jináb-i-Fádil-i-Shírází and for his spouse, Naw-Zuhúr Khánum, as well as copies of some of Fádil's letters to the Master, and other pertinent documents. Words cannot express my deep sense of gratitude to that August Body for its careful review, impeccable correction and final approval of the provisional translations I submitted, eighteen in all, most of which are included in this book.

My special thanks are due to my dear friend Ehsán Erfánífar who kindly offered and undertook the task of translating into English the above-mentioned Tablets, thereby providing me with my first set of provisional translations.

I am also grateful to those who responded to my request and shared with me their remembrances of Jináb-i-Fádil, particularly to those whose contribution I have chosen to include in the book, Dr.'Izzatu'lláh Azízí, Dr. Iraj Ayman and a former student of Fádil who wished to remain anonymous.

ACKNOWLEDGEMENTS

I am grateful to my cousin Mojgán Fáregh who provided me with several photographs and documents belonging to her mother Rúháníyyih (Fádil's youngest daughter) and to my brother Farámarz Faláhi who assisted in preparing them for use in this book. I am deeply thankful to Don Brown who helped enormously with his guidance, technical assistance and advice. My warm appreciation also goes to my daughter Anísá for helping with photos and typing a portion of the manuscript's original draft, and to Darlene Gait for her help with digitalizing some of the photographs.

A special and sincere thanks must go to all those friends and family members whose encouraging words helped sustain me throughout the long course of the book's development.

Finally, I would express my gratitude for the constant assistance and encouragement of my husband Bill, without whose continued involvement in the overall formatting, editing and polishing process the book in its final appearance would not have been possible.

Preface

In a conversation with Counsellor Hidáyatu'lláh (Hedi) Aḥmadíyyih* during the 1988 International Convention in Haifa, Israel, I was urged by him to write the biography of my grandfather, Jináb-i-Fádil-i-Shírází. As we spoke it occurred to me that there were no doubt many other early believers in Írán whose exemplary services and heroic sacrifices for their beloved Faith had not been adequately documented and published, and that writing my grandfather's story was something I should consider. Fascinating accounts of him, given me by my mother and grandmother began to fill my head, accounts of his relentless search for truth, of his unique, lengthy and arduous means to

---

* This devoted servant of Bahá'u'lláh and outstanding teacher of the Faith served as a Counsellor in Central America for over a decade. He and his family resided in Belize where he also carried on a medical practice. His colourfully illustrated teaching manual was used extensively throughout the Americas in several different languages. One night in 1989, while returning from one of his teaching trips in a neighbouring country, he fell to his death while attempting, in pitch dark, to cross a bridge which was under repair.

attain the object of his longing, discovering through his own efforts the identity of his beloved ('Abdu'l-Bahá), of eventually attaining His presence and there becoming the recipient of true knowledge and understanding, then of his years of sacrificial service as an outstanding teacher of the Cause. My grandfather had passed to the next world before I or any of his grandchildren knew him, but it was from hearing my mother and my grandmother speak of him that I knew him to have been a very humble man, self-effacing and completely detached from this transitory world.

Heartened by the Counsellor's words and aware of the story's merit, it was not long before my decision was made to take up the challenge of writing it.

Dr. Aḥmad'iyyih encouraged me to see if I could obtain from the World Centre copies of the original Tablets of 'Abdu'l-Bahá revealed in honour of my grandfather plus any other relevant information that might be there. I discussed the matter briefly with Mr. 'Alí Nakhjavání during that Convention and it was through his kind assistance that I began to communicate with the Universal House of Justice. Eventually, much to my delight and with a deep sense of gratitude, I received copies of eighteen Tablets of the Master addressed to Fádil and four of Fádil's letters sent to the Master. Most of the Tablets, in the form of provisional translations approved by the House of Justice, are included in this book. I would very much like to have been able to include copies of the beloved Guardian's letters to Fádil plus examples of Fádil's surviving poems and song lyrics but alas, because they had been hidden along with his writings and books during the 1979 Islámic Revolution in Írán and remain there in an undisclosed place, I unfortunately had no access to them.

Enthusiasm carried me through the book's initial stages of researching the Master's Tablets, writing to individuals for information and beginning the work of translating into English some material on Fádil which had been written in Persian. However my family and I had been pioneering in Costa Rica from 1980 and, because of my involvement in Bahá'í administration at local and national levels and in a variety of projects, I had little time for the book. It was not until after returning to Canada in 1998 that it became possible for me to resume work on it.

The writing process was well along when I received from the beloved Hand of the Cause Jináb-i-Varqá, himself once a devoted student of Fádil, encouraging words that confirmed my resolve to carry the work to completion. In his letter he refers to Fádil as, "...my beloved teacher..." and affirms, "Indeed it is a wonderful idea to collect the memories of this great servant of Bahá'u'lláh, as the present generation is deprived of having sufficient information regarding his life and the great services which he rendered in the teaching field."

It is one of my hopes that the story of Jináb-i-Fádil-i-Shírází will prove fascinating and inspirational to, among others, the generation of Iranian Bahá'ís and their children who have lived outside Írán all of their lives but whose grandparents and great grandparents grew up in Írán and endured difficulties and restricted circumstances similar to those experienced by my grandfather. Another hope is that the biography will encourage those who have descended from believers whose personal lives and exemplary service to the Faith can be a source of inspiration to the present and subsequent generations of Bahá'ís, to undertake documenting the lives of their eminent ancestors.

I feel relieved and satisfied knowing that my task has been accomplished but it would give me great joy if I could know that readers were finding the book not only engaging but inspiring as well; I venture to hope this will be so.

Houri Faláhi-Skuce
Shawnigan Lake, BC
October 20th, 2003

Introduction

Much of the biographical information on Jináb-i-
Fádil contained in this book is based on accounts that
my grandfather himself had related to his wife and
children. His wife, Naw-Zuhúr Khánum, shared many
stories of Fádil's life experiences with Jináb-i-Azízu'lláh
Sulaymání, a scholar and author who wrote a biographical work in Persian consisting of several volumes and was entitled Maṣábih-i-Hidáyat (Lamps of
Guidance).

I remember from childhood Mr. Sulaymání having
several interviews with my grandmother for the purpose of gathering information to write an account of
Jináb-i-Fádil's life and work in the first volume of his
biographical series; what he wrote has been an invalu-
able source of information to me in writing this book.

In the first part of the book my grandfather is referred to by his given name, Ibráhím. After the title Fádil
(Learned) is bestowed upon him by 'Abdu'l-Bahá he is
referred to as Jináb-i-Fádil or Fádil (pronounced Fá·zel´).

In Persian culture, the word Jináb is used to address
a distinguished individual; it means, "His Honour".

In chapters twenty-two and twenty-three, where
Fádil's spouse is introduced, there is mention made of

Fá'izih Khánum, the aunt who raised her. I have included in the Appendix a brief account of Fá'izih Khánum's eventful and exemplary life as a tribute to her heroic services to the Cause.

All Persian and Arabic names are transliterated in accordance with the system adopted for books of the Bahá'í Faith. Most dates mentioned in this book are according to the Muslim lunar (AH) calendar followed by the Gregorian (AD) calendar. In a few instances the dates available to me are written according to the Muslim solar calendar followed by an equivalent Gregorian date.

Verses taken from the Qur'án are numbered in accordance with what is given in the English translated version entitled, "Qur'án-i-Karím", The Noble Qur'án, by Dr. Muḥammad-Taqí-ud-Dín Al-Hilátí and Dr. Muḥammad-Muḥsin Khán, 1419 AH edition, Madinah, K.S.A. and are listed in the "Notes & References".

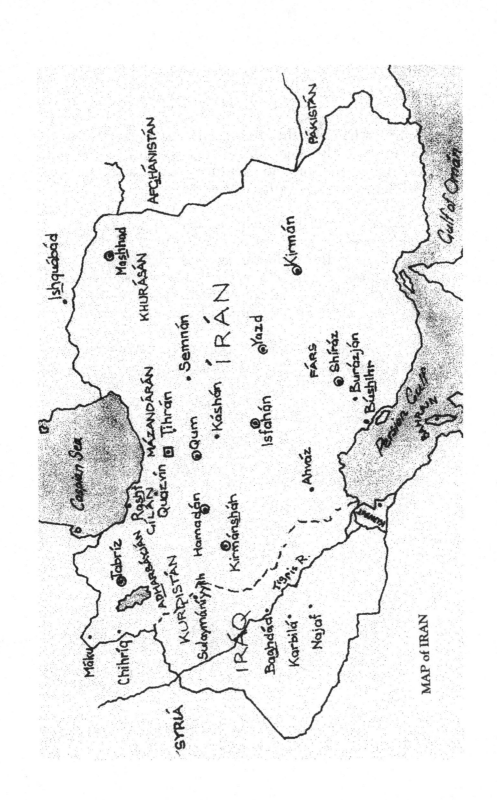

MAP of IRAN

One

Ancestors

During the first century of the Islámic dispensation (the early 700's A.D.) holy war in the Middle East was being waged by Arabian Muslim armies. The people of Persia (now known as Írán)[1] belonged to the Zoroastrian Faith and when conquest came to Persia (637-641A.D.) many Zoroastrian clans left to settle in neighbouring lands, especially India, rather than remain in Persia and be forced to convert to Islám. The ancestors of Shaykh Muḥammad-Ibráhím Fádil-i-Shírází, who were then residing in the southern province of Fárs, were among the hundreds who gave up their homes and struck out for safety beyond the reach of Islámic encroachment. It was travelling en route to India that, while camped on the Island of Bahrain in the Persian Gulf, they encountered envoys of the Imám 'Alí, the cousin and son-in-law of the Prophet Muḥammad, His lawful successor, who had come to that island with the mission of proclaiming the Message of Islám to its inhabitants. Thus Muḥammad-Ibráhím's ancestors became first acquainted with, then enamoured of the new teachings and at length converted to Shí'ah Islám.

1

Having embraced the young Faith they had been attempting to flee, they decided to remain on Bahrain, restore a degree of domestic normality to their lives and seek prosperity under the protection and guidance provided by their new Faith, Islám. Remaining its followers, succeeding generations continued to serve the Faith with devotion and ardour. Eventually, the island was invaded and taken over by members of the Wahhábí sect, a movement that had sprung from the Sunní sect of Islám but rejected many of its traditions. Muḥammad-Ibn-i-'Abd-i'l-Wahháb, a native of Najd in Arabia, founded this sect in the early seventeenth century. Muḥammad-Ibráhím's ancestors, who could not tolerate living under the rule of the Wahhábis, left Bahrain and returned to the land their ancestors had fled several centuries before, resettling in the Province of Fárs in the vicinity of its capital city, Shíráz.

The history of Fárs goes back to the beginning of the Persian Empire when the first Persians, or Pársís, came to settle in the area. It extended over much of the southern region of what is now known as Írán. During the Achaemenian and Sássánián Dynasties, 559-330 BC & 224-637AD respectively, great cities such as the famous Persepolis and Estakhr were built there. The magnificent ruins of Persepolis still exist among the desert mountains at the edge of a fertile valley, a reminder of the greatness of Persia some twenty-five hundred years ago.

Following the Arab conquest and the fall of the Sássánián dynasty, their last capital city, Estakhr, gradually fell into decline. Shíráz, which began only as a settlement, grew into an important regional centre

2

during Sássánián rule. It increased in size and importance under the Arabs (637-1050AD) and became the Provincial Capital, rivalling even the great city of Baghdád which was founded in the late eighth century AD.

When Muḥammad-Ibráhim's ancestors returned to Fárs, the Zand dynasty ruled Persia (1747-79) and Shíráz was the nation's capital. It is the birthplace of the great Persian poets Háfíz and Sa'di and was a leading centre of the arts and home to many brilliant artists, scholars, calligraphers and architects during the 13th and 14th century. It was during the reign of Áqá Muḥammad Khán, founder of the Qájár dynasty (1779-1797), that the national capital was moved to Ṭihrán.

Two

A Strange Dream

The lineage of <u>Sh</u>ay<u>kh</u> Muḥammad-Ibráhim's renowned ancestral predecessors is rich in sages, mystics and scholars who distinguished themselves, especially in the areas of theology and religious jurisprudence and whose diligence, study and research led to their authoring many outstanding literary works. Notable among those who thus adorn the family tree was <u>Sh</u>ay<u>kh</u> Najaf 'Alí, the father of Muḥammad-Ibráhím, a prominent mujtahid (Muslim doctor of law) of the town of Burázján in the province of Fárs.

The <u>Sh</u>ay<u>kh</u> had two wives, both of widely known and esteemed families. Marriage to his second wife occurred after his brother's death when the <u>Sh</u>ay<u>kh</u>, following custom, married his brother's widow Maryam and extended protection and care to the bereaved family by taking them into his household.

While Muḥammad-Ibráhím's mother was pregnant with him the <u>Sh</u>ay<u>kh</u> experienced a curious dream; it involved both wives and occurred at a time when both women were pregnant. In it he saw the Prophet Abraham, in the figure of a small child, sitting on his lap.

4

Suddenly he became a grown man who outshone the Shaykh in the maturity of his powers both mental and spiritual. The grown child addressed the astonished Shaykh saying, "I wish to remain in your family". Upon awakening the Shaykh interpreted the amazing dream to mean that a special and unusual boy would be born to one of his two wives. He waited expectantly. When his first wife gave birth to a baby girl he knew that the child born to Maryam would be a boy.

It was the year 1279 of the Muslim calendar (1863), when the day arrived. As it was customary in those days that a special smooth mixture with honey and butter be given to newborns, the Shaykh had instructed that no one should give nourishment to the child; he himself would administer the sweet mixture. The attendants, realizing it was a boy, washed and clothed the infant then summoned the boy's father. The Shaykh hastened at once to his newborn son, took him gently in his arms and, tenderly embracing the child, fed him the mixture. Gazing upon the infant's features and becoming aware they were those of the child in his dream, his heart filled with the strength and glow of paternal love and, certain that his dream had been a divine mandate of conferral, he gave his new son the name Ibráhím (Abraham).

Since Shaykh Najaf 'Alí was a man of considerable wealth the young Ibráhím had the good fortune to spend his early years enjoying not only the love, care and endearing affection of his parents but the benefits and luxuries afforded by the family's wealth.

Schooling began for him when he reached the age
of seven; with a turban on his head and the words,
"Salám va Salavát" (Praise and greetings to God,
Muḥammad and His descendents) ringing in his ears,
he was sent off to school to be educated.

After two years of instruction in Persian, he began
his studies in Arabic, a challenging and difficult language to master even for the best of scholars. Progres-
sing rapidly, Ibráhím gained an extraordinary command of it within the relatively short space of three
years.

By the time he reached the age of twelve, Ibráhím's
older half brother Shaykh Ḥusayn had for some time
been studying in Shíráz. Ibráhím, eager to avail himself of the same opportunity, asked his father if he
might join his brother and continue his studies there
also. When Shaykh Najaf 'Alí consented, the boy was
enrolled at Mushír School in Shíráz and was moved
into the same quarters his brother occupied.

Although the exact number of Ibráhím's siblings is
not known, it is clear that he had at least one brother,
one sister, four half brothers and one half sister. Each
year during the holidays Ibráhím and his brother
would return to Burázján to visit their family. Shaykh
Ḥusayn eventually left the school and Ibráhím, retain-
ing the quarters they had shared, continued on as the
sole occupant.

Three

The Knowledge-Hungry Student

Soon after his arrival in Shíráz Ibráhím began a search for the best theology teachers under whom he might begin his studies. He had heard that the most prestigious theological college in Shíráz was Madrisih-i-Khán so one day he set out to go there for a visit and to make inquiries about its professors.

The college was named after Imám Qulí Khán, a former Governor of Fárs Province who had founded the college in 1615. This serene training seminary had a fine stone-walled inner courtyard set around a garden. Entrance to the building was through a very impressive portal with an unusual type of stalactite moulding inside the outer arch and very intricate mosaic tiling in the inner doorway. In spite of the extensive damage by earthquakes, a small part of the college building remains to this day, situated in the famous Bázár district of Shíráz.

"I recall the day Ibráhím arrived at the school yard as an obvious newcomer", recalled Jináb-i-Vaḥíd Kashfí, already a student at the school and one who, some years later, embraced the Bahá'í Faith and went

7

on to become a distinguished and knowledgeable Bahá'í. "I was seated with two friends in the yard outside our classroom at the Khán School. We called the handsome young Ibráhím over to us and asked him who he was and what he had come for. He introduced himself as Shaykh Ibráhím and said he was there to continue his theological studies. When we asked in what field he readily replied, 'In the field of religious jurisprudence, its doctrines, methods and principles'. He added that he was looking for a good professor who taught what he wanted, whereupon my friends and I named some reputable theologians who were teaching at the Khán School. Then I ventured, 'If you are interested in philosophy I could introduce you to Mullá 'Abbás, an erudite researcher in the field'.

"As soon as this serious young man from Burázján heard mention of philosophy his boyish brow wrinkled in a thoughtful expression before he replied with earnest misgiving, 'They tell me that philosophy takes you away from religion and turns you into an infidel'. The ironic nature of his brash speculation caused my friends and I to burst into laughter".

Several years later at the age of eighteen, Muḥammad-Ibráhím had completed his studies of religious jurisprudence and, in fact, did commence studies in philosophy. He enrolled under the recommended Mullá 'Abbás, himself a former student of the renowned Mullá Ḥádí-i-Sabzivárí. A few years later, with these intense studies behind him, the knowledge-hungry youth turned his absorbent intellect toward a two year program of science, more philosophy, some logic and also mysticism, completing

8

it under the able tutelage of, among others, Mírzá Áqá-i-Jahromí.

The Mayor of S͟híráz, who was also the owner of the Mus͟hír school, made a practice of periodic trips to check on the tullȧb (theology students) and would always seek out Muḥammad-Ibráhím for a chat, not only because his philosophy professor had praised his talent and aptitude for learning but also because of the young man's warm presence, friendly disposition and likeable manner.

Mus͟híru'l-Mulk, as the Mayor was called, had no offspring of his own but had adopted his wife's young sister and raised her like his own child. Because he had grown fond of Muḥammad-Ibráhím he entertained a hope that the young student would marry the girl and thus become even more like a son to him. Over a period of time, aware of the young man's great taste for books, the Mayor had lavished him with as many as three hundred quality volumes. To the same end he had given him furniture of exquisite quality for his living quarters along with several qalyáns (hubble bubble pipes²), each tastefully fitted with a silver head and base. Whenever he would visit, the Mayor would use remarks calculated to stimulate thoughts of marriage in the mind of his young friend, but they gained less than an encouraging response. Typically, for example, a statement employed by the mayor such as, "You have everything here except a wife," would, from Muḥammad-Ibráhím, whose mind was far from his own material well being and a comfortable family life, evoke nothing but silence.

9

Four

Arduous Search

During those days a humble shoe salesman by the name of Muḥammad-Káẓim made the rounds to schools in Shíráz on a regular basis selling his 'giveh' (hand woven cotton summer shoes) of many different colours and sizes. Muḥammad-Ibráhím would enjoy pleasant conversations with the visiting merchant who, although a humble and uneducated man, would speak in a profound and mystic manner, something the young student found strangely attractive.

Had he known that Muḥammad-Káẓim, who never spoke of his deeply held beliefs, was in reality a Bahá'í he would undoubtedly have perceived the shoe vendor much differently. Ibráhím's state, one of devotion, asceticism, piety and whole-hearted adherence to the Shí'ah message of Islám, would have given rise to such aversion that it would, most assuredly have prevented him from socializing with Káẓim; in fact he would, unhesitatingly, have driven Káẓim away.

Back then Bahá'ís were called Bábís. The term Bábí was an appellation given to the followers of the Báb (Gate), the Prophet-Herald of the Bahá'í Faith. The

10

masses of people continued to call the followers of
Bahá'u'lláh by that term until gradually, in the early
1900's, with the opening of Bahá'í schools and a
hospital and the visits of Bahá'í educators, nurses and
physicians from Europe and America, the word Bábí
was replaced by Bahá'í. Only a handful that remained
followers of Mírzá Yaḥyá[3] were called Bábís, or Azalís
after his title Subh-i-Azal.

It was due to a Shí'ah Muslim belief that all non-
Muslims were unclean infidels, (in a religious not a
physical sense) that Muslims came to regard the Bábís
as unclean. It stemmed from a misinterpretation by
their clergy of a verse in the Qur'án which states, "O
ye who believe in Alláh's Oneness and in His Messenger Muḥammad! Verily the mushrikun (idolaters, dis-
believers in the Oneness of Alláh and the Message of
Muḥammad) are najasun (unclean)."[4] Later it became
common belief that the verse refers also to the followers of all other Faiths. So for a devout Muslim like
Muḥammad-Ibráhím, the mere thought of Bábís, or
Bahá'ís, would call forth the need to repeat, "Astaqfur
Alláh", a request for God's forgiveness.

Some years later when Ibráhím, this diligent and
devoted student of Islám, would recognize and embrace the Bahá'í Faith, he would realize the influential
effect towards this end that his association with
Muḥammad-Káẓim had had. He would, as well,
appreciate the importance Bahá'u'lláh, the Founder of
his new Faith, placed on promoting love and unity
amongst all mankind by exhorting his followers to,
"Consort with the followers of all religions in a spirit
of friendliness and fellowship", and by pronouncing

11

that, "Whatsoever hath led the children of men to shun one another, and hath caused dissensions and divisions amongst men hath, through the revelation of these words, been nullified and abolished."[5]

At the age of twenty Muḥammad-Ibráhím had completed his formal studies, which included a variety of sciences and had already earned much recognition and distinction for his erudition. But he was not concerned with the accolades, for a new preoccupation had seized his restless mind, the working through of which would profoundly alter his destiny.

His thought, already steeped in and shaped by a broad array of spiritual poetry, discourses and treatises of some of Islám's pre-eminent mystics and philosophers during his years of formal education, was now to become more directly influenced by his studies in theosophy. This discipline proposes through contemplation, meditation, revelation etc., to establish direct contact with divine principle for the purpose of gaining spiritual insight, a treasure regarded as more desirable than and superior to empirical knowledge.

An overwhelming desire took hold of him, fuelled by youthful spiritual ambition in its full glow and folly. Under its sway he determined to establish as his goal, the station of prophet-hood, reasoning, "If the prophets, those essences of detachment, and revealers of Holy Books, though apparently individual human beings, had been able to reach the station of prophethood, why then is it not possible for me to attain it as well?"

This preoccupation caused Muḥammad-Ibráhím much turmoil and mental anguish. From then on, blind to the fact that prophet-hood is not a chosen vocation, that God appoints his prophets, they do not appoint themselves nor do they attain prophet-hood as a rank through striving and study, he spent his days and nights oblivious to all but one flaming issue, that of his quest. So scattered and distressed were his thoughts at times, so distracted his state of mind, that he forgot food and sleep, missed meals and was often found absent from his room at night.

Detached from everything but his books he continued reading inordinately; however the agitation and excitement precipitated by this practice plus the imbalanced state he had managed to achieve on all levels of his life, eventually caused him to suffer a condition in which ultimately, he was even unable to read.

At last it occurred to Muḥammad-Ibráhím that standing between him and the realization of his sublime quest was attachment, inordinate or otherwise, to his trove of beloved books, those volumes which he had revered as precious repositories of truth, custodians of great thought and the wellsprings of his ever-expanding knowledge; volumes which had nourished his thinking, inspired his spirit, stimulated his mind and set his heart upon the great and lofty objective which now inflamed in his soul and enveloped his being.

Once convinced that what stood in his way were his books and that the final step to complete detachment for him meant disencumbering himself of this last great obstacle, he resolutely proceeded to carry them all out of his room into the school courtyard, heave them into a stack, douse them with gasoline, set the pile ablaze and watch with anxious, silent resolve as flames reduced them to ashes.

The book-burning occurrence, although succeeding in tangibly stripping Muḥammad-Ibráhím of his last vestige of material attachment, left him, alas, unsatisfied that he was any closer to achieving his goal. Many a day he spent in confusion until finally the day came when his soul began to perceive a slight glimmer of hope. There was yet one aspect of the physical world from which he had not yet broken the shackles. Desperately he thought, "I have cut myself from everything except my physical body, surely it is attachment to this which remains the obstacle for my attainment to all truth."

Then in his heart there began to move and be heard the mystical rhythms of the eminent fourteenth century poet whose songs and verse have become the treasured jewels adorning the ancient edifice of Persian culture. "Do not look for the essence of love from the school's corner", came the words of Háfíz. "Step out from there if you desire to find it."

The words continued to echo in his mind until he at last reached a decision. Approaching his younger brother who had been attending the school and sharing Ibráhím's living space since midway through the duration of his years in Shíráz, he handed him the keys to their 'hojrah' (living quarters) and told him that he would be spending the evening at a dinner party and might not return. "You had better have these keys," said Ibráhím, sensing that indeed he might not return, but not because a dinner party prevented him.

Five

A Mystical Experience

It was an hour or two past midday when Ibráhím left the school and departed the city on foot. Five or six hours later with the sun low in the sky and not having yet reached the holy shrine, Haft Tan, he came upon a pack of wild dogs devouring an animal carcass by the side of the road. Wary of his approach several dogs broke off to chase him barking viciously and growling so menacingly that, terror-struck, he fainted to the ground.

But while he lay there on the ground in a state of unconsciousness he experienced something extraordinary. As though in a dream, he was able, from the top of a tree, to look down on his body, a thing to which he seemed no longer attached, except perhaps by feelings of resentment.

In the world of spirit, travel is not hindered by the kind of restrictions we are subject to in the time world of materiality, so the instant Ibráhím was reminded of the longing he had been harbouring for complete detachment from his body he was, at the speed of thought, transported to a place more beautiful, many times over, than any he had ever experienced. As he gazed in awe and wonder he felt greatly attracted by it. However, an encroaching thought of his physical frame, with the same speed, returned him to the tree-top from where he again could observe his motionless body. Repugnance and aversion filled him once more but just then he recalled the wondrous words which had spurred him to embark on his journey in the first place: 'Step out from there if you desire to find it!' whereupon the clear recollection of the words freed him. As they continued to echo through the corridors of his spirit he became fixated with their sublime significance, but again he lost hold and was again returned to beholding his unmoving corporeal frame from the treetop vantage point and re-experiencing his initial and intense disgust of it.

A third time, upon experiencing complete detachment from his body his spirit attempted to reach that beautifully adorned and most sublime world. At once, as a mysterious voice was heard to say, "This is your rank and abode," he began to perceive an indescribable place. "If you should attempt to reach this place now," said the voice, "your efforts will not avail; you must prepare by returning to the world below wherein your development is to be completed. This is necessary. In your haste to attain you have reached here too soon; at the age of seventy-two you will ascend." In that moment, what Ibráhím had been experiencing as a state of sublime exaltation suddenly changed and, becoming acutely aware of his spiritual pretensions and the delusions he had been labouring under, he was met with a profound sense of regret and remorse.

Coming to without warning he found himself back in his body, sitting on a sun-drenched patch of overgrown grass, shoeless and bareheaded. He sat up and, finding himself unscathed, assumed that the dogs must have merely sniffed him over then scampered back to resume feeding or to find a bone they could make off with. Struggling to his feet he located his shoes, found his turban, dusted himself off and started back towards town.

Noting as he travelled that the sun had not yet reached its meridian, he soon realized that he was not returning on the day he had set out but the day following and that many hours had lapsed during his time of "unconsciousness" when he had experienced such astounding things.

Ibráhím, determined that his efforts henceforth would be adjusted to the insights and new understandings he had been given, began to practice with vigour a spiritual discipline of prayer, fasting and the chanting of certain holy verses and exhortations known as the riázat. According to the belief of notables within the Islámic Faith, the one who practiced such would be led to behold the countenance of the promised Qá'im and receive the bounty of recognizing Him.

From time to time he would be invited, along with other 'tulláb's' (theological students), to a dinner party at the home of Mushíru'l-Mulk. Initially he decided not to attend. At the end of the afternoon on each day the feast was to occur he would make sure that everyone else had gone by checking for unlocked doors and questioning anyone who had remained behind. He

17

adopted the practice of quietly remaining in his room after sunset, seated with the door locked, lest the Mushíru'l-Mulk should unwittingly rouse him.

Eventually Ibráhím decided that such practice was not sufficiently challenging. It was too easy to refrain from eating when one could not see the food; it would be better to attend the banquets and abstain from eating with the food in front of him. So he began attending the dinner parties where the appetizing colours and delicious aromas of the cooked dishes were far more tempting in their immediacy. Rather than allowing a desire to partake to gain ascendancy in him Ibráhím would refrain from serving himself but pass the food to whomever happened to be seated next to him, helping himself only to some noon va sabzí (bread and herbs).

His efforts along this pathway of self-denial proved successful; as his practice continued he felt more purified in heart and able to discover the secrets of many intricate and hitherto baffling matters. His assurance grew and, with fresh resurgence, he confidently proceeded along the evermore certain path of his spiritual attainment.

Although he was not yet twenty-four, some important relationships were about to develop which would prove to be of great help in furthering his spiritual aspirations.

Six

In the Company of a Dervish

In those days there was a man from Shíráz named 'Abdu'l-Hamid who was widely known as a mystic and a wise man. He had suffered greatly by cruel and unjust treatment at the hands of the former governor of Shíráz and because of it he eventually was obliged to give up his home and possessions and leave the city. Doing so he retired to the seclusion of a holy place near Shíráz known as the Haft Tan (the Seven Sleepers of Ephesus) where he was content to occupy, along with a few dervishes who became his devotees, a cold, dark, semi-underground corner within it.

'Abdu'l-Hamid, knew Ibráhím and had recognized his sincerity and purity of heart. He was also aware of his spiritual orientation and pursuit of the mystic's ultimate goal. Having decided to lend him assistance in attaining his objective, 'Abdu'l-Hamid sent one of his disciples, Shaykh Muhammad-Taqí, with instructions to bring Ibráhím to see him.

As it was their first meeting the Shaykh felt a little awkward about approaching Ibráhím with his "mission" so he decided to open the conversation by requesting a service. Carrying with him the pages of an

19

old contract, the S͟hayk͟h approached Muḥammad-
Ibráhím and asked if he would write, on his behalf, a
petition to the governor concerning the contract.
Ibráhím, liking his honest and gentle appearance, was
quick however to discern that the S͟hayk͟h's visit was
for other reasons. "Of course", he said to him, reveal-
ing his discernment, "all this is a pretext; why don't
you tell me the real reason you are here?"

The S͟hayk͟h acknowledged his attempt at deception
then replied truthfully, "I have been sent by 'Abdu'l-
Ḥamid who wishes to see you and in fact," he added
humbly but with disguised relish, "he summons you to
his presence at the Ḥaft Tan".

Ibráhím, carefully considering the S͟hayk͟h's words,
sensed in them a spiritual imperative.

The next day he set out for the Ḥaft Tan and got
there an hour or so before 'Abdu'l-Ḥamid. When the
venerable teacher arrived from the fields in his flowing
white beard and dressed in the garb of a dervish, he
greeted Ibráhím with a warm smile then, with move-
ments and gestures in place of words, welcomed him
to his humble dwelling.

Thus began a remarkable encounter for with no
word spoken but by means of gestures and signs the
import of mystical allusions was conveyed to Ibráhím's
understanding. Soon he knew in his heart the spiritual
quest of recognizing his Lord would no longer be served by an approach of strict discipline and the self-
infliction of bodily hardships and deprivations. He
was thus brought to realize that now the pathway
which would lead to the truth of reality and the knowledge of his Lord would have to be an inward spiritual

journey, one that would produce for him the refinement of soul needed for the striving, seeking and searching which would now be required of him.

Over the course of a full year the two continued to meet periodically and converse silently in this way. By virtue of their intuitive powers, many states and disclosures of spiritual truth were experienced by them during such meetings; meetings characterized by deep meditation, reflection and spiritual discovery. Although silent, the two men communicated, now in stillness, now by the use of signs. In those moments 'Abdu'l-Ḥamid would assist Ibráhím to "see", with a growing inward awareness of their station, the resplendent and luminous personages of His Holiness the Báb, the Blessed Beauty, Bahá'u'lláh and His Holiness, 'Abdu'l-Bahá. It was many years later that Ibráhím was to learn the true identity of 'Abdu'l-Ḥamid and become aware that he was one who had attained the presence of Bahá'u'lláh during His sojourn in Sulaymáníyyih.

The day arrived when Ibráhím sensed that his fruitful time with 'Abdu'l-Ḥamid was drawing to a close. He knew that now, with patience as his steed and in a state of complete resignation, he would have to travel alone into the valley of search to any or all regions in search of the Beloved. Sensing this also, 'Abdu'l-Ḥamid assured him in spoken words that he was now sufficiently accomplished spiritually and knowledgeable enough to embark upon the next stage of his quest. He followed with, "You are now ready. I have entrusted Muḥammad-Taqí with a small package for you; be good enough to pick it up from him on the day of your departure."

When that day arrived Muḥammad-Taqí, faithful to the instructions of 'Abdu'l-Ḥamid, came to Ibráhím with a small parcel. It contained a miraculous substance, the result of 'Abdu'l-Ḥamid's discovery in the science of alchemy. It was in fact 'Kímiá', a reddish powder which, when applied to copper, transmutes it into pure gold. Muḥammad-Taqí, opened the parcel, demonstrated the method of applying the elixir, then rebundled it, handed it to Ibráhím and left. From the time he received it and throughout his journey to the Holy Land, the powder remained among Ibráhím's precious things. He was to eventually discard it without ever having used it.

Seven

En Route to Khurásán

Departing Shíráz with a firm sense of purpose, he made directly for Burázján to visit his family. There, without telling his father of his sublime spiritual quest, Ibráhím indicated that he would like to visit the Atabát-i-Álíát, the holy shrines of the Imáms at Najaf and Karbilá. These are two cities in Iráq and are places of pilgrimage for the Shí'ah sect of Islám. In Karbilá is the shrine of the martyred Imám Husayn, his brother Abbás and the Imám's young martyred son, 'Alí-Akbar. In Najaf is the shrine of the Imám 'Alí, son-in-law and rightful successor to the Prophet Muhammad the first of the twelve Imáms. He explained to his father that he needed to stay a while in those cities in order to complete his studies. Ibráhím's father, who had always, with understanding, acceded to his son's wishes, agreed with his decision and gave him funds sufficient to meet his travel and living expenses.

Soon after he arrived in the vicinity of the two cities he settled in and enrolled in classes of theology and religious jurisprudence under the instruction of a renowned mujtahid named Mullá Kázim-i-Khurásání. In

23

addition to what he gained from the courses, there was much opportunity for him to learn through interacting with other scholars also studying under the mujtahid. While his well-established practice of worship and contemplation never faltered, his soul continued to gather in and treasure every new spiritual discovery and his mind to ponder things of great import. Hence, throughout the period of his stay in Karbilá and Najaf, Ibráhím's knowledge continued to increase and his understanding to deepen.

At length Ibráhím's brother, Shaykh Muḥammad-Ḥassan, at the behest of their father, arrived in Najaf to continue his own studies and to keep Ibráhím company. But it was not long after his brother's arrival that Ibráhím had a dream and in it he was told that his search would soon lead him to the province of Khurásán. The very next morning, not wanting to explain to his brother the nature of his quest nor his vehement longing to find the treasure he sought, he informed his brother that he would be gone for a couple of weeks on a pilgrimage to the tomb of one of the Imám's descendents. He gave his brother the keys to their quarters and, taking with him a few pieces of clothing and several items he would need, set out on foot; awaiting him, Khurásán, that beautiful province in the northeast of Írán with its lush scenery and its capital, Mashhad.

While his journey would take him through Ṭihrán it was on his way there that he gained a travelling companion, a dervish who, after they reached the city, went his own way leaving Ibráhím to continue on alone. It later became known to him that the dervish

24

who had journeyed alongside him was one of seven dervishes who had recognized Bahá'u'lláh and embraced His Faith.

Among some of the extraordinary things Ibráhím experienced during the six months it took him from the time he left Najaf until he reached Mashhad, was an incident that occurred while he was passing through the rugged mountains en route. He had reached a caravanserai after a day's walk and had spent the night bedded down by a wall. The next day he awoke at dawn and proceeded toward the foot of a nearby mountain. As he got closer he could see in the distance light from a small fire. Proceeding toward it he suddenly heard a voice piercing the morning shadows in a demanding tone, "Who goes there?" said the voice then ordered, "Stop where you are!" Ibráhím froze. A man brandishing a weapon approached him from behind and indicated that he should walk ahead of him towards the mountain in the direction of the fire he had seen.

As he got close to the fire he could see by its light a group of armed men, whom he realized were highwaymen and bandits, sitting around the fire drinking tea. One, who appeared to be the leader, said in a loud voice that rang with authority, "Where are you coming from? Where are you going? What have you got with you?" Ibráhím answered to the point, "I come from 'Atabát-i-Áliat, I am headed for Khurásán and I am carrying nothing." A man was ordered to search him and, when only a few coins were found, they realized he had spoken the truth. Thinking him a dervish they told him he could sit and join them for tea.

Some time later, as the sun was beginning to appear above the distant mountain, Ibráhím noticed a big pot on the fire alive with bubbles and full to the brim; it contained stew from a large fat lamb, killed and set to boil in the early morning. Around noon it was brought from the fire and, when invited to stay for lunch, Ibráhím gladly accepted.

Seated among the unlikely band of companions, he enjoyed his meal with great relish, so much so that years later he was able to recall vividly the flavour of that delicious lamb stew. As he was about to depart, his hosts gathered up some left over meat and, along with two loaves of bread, some tea and a half kilo of sugar, handed it to him for sustenance over the remainder of his journey. He thanked them and bid them farewell.

Eight

More Dreams

Mashhad, the capital city of <u>Kh</u>urásán Province in northeastern Írán, is well known as a place of pilgrimage for the <u>Sh</u>í'ah Muslims. Located there is the holy tomb of the Imám Riḍá, eighth in the line of successors, called Imáms, stemming from the Prophet Muḥammad. It was to this shrine that Ibráhím made several visits and performed the required ceremonies. It was there that he waited in great hope and anticipation, searching, meditating, praying that he would soon see the fulfillment of what he had dreamed in Najaf.

During this time of waiting he had another dream of great significance in which he saw himself in the company of the Imám Riḍá, the two of them ascending toward the throne of the Almighty. There were three great figures; the central one he was immediately able to identify as the Almighty Creator, the other two, flanking the central figure on either side were, he realized, the two exalted beings nearest to the Creator. As Ibráhím watched, the Almighty handed to one of the figures a book indicating it be given to Ibráhím to correct. Upon receiving it he realized, because the book was voluminous and its contents lengthy and detailed, he would not have time just then to accomplish his assigned task and made a remark to that effect. He then heard the voice of the Lord telling him to keep the book and, when the right time arrived, he could make the corrections.

Just fifty days following that dream Ibráhím experienced another; in it he again saw one of the great prophets and this time his heart was rejoiced with these words, "Indeed you shall see the Haq (the truth) in this world, however not here but in Burázján". This, of course, was where his family lived. With a great sense of expectancy and again on foot he set out for the home he had left a few years earlier, returning to it after a journey of several months.

Nine

A Return Home

His parents had been told by Ibráhím's brother of his failure to return or send word and were in despair that they would ever learn of his whereabouts. They were at first of course overjoyed to see him but it was not long before his father was unable to hide his dissatisfaction over the changes wrought in his son through his ascetic disciplines, his rigorous abstinence from earthly pleasures and his changed thinking. Shaykh Najaf-'Alí had for so long held to the hope that his son would one day gain fame, power and respect in the community like the other theologians and mullás of his time. But Ibráhím, to his father's great disappointment, displayed no ambition for leadership or for acquiring a name or a high position among his peers.

It was not long before Shaykh Najaf-'Alí arrived at the decision that marriage would be the remedy for his son. However, contemplating the wisdom of such a decision, it did not occur to him that the most likely candidate for Ibráhím's betrothed would be the daughter of another Shaykh.

Shaykh Muḥammad-Ḥassan was an influential mujtahid in the town and, through his opposition and
influence, had always been a rival of Ibráhím's father;
on the surface, although friendly and respectful towards him, he strove against him and regarded him as
a competitor.

It was not long after his return that Ibráhím was
paid a visit by the Shaykh, an act according to custom
he was obliged to return. On the day he returned the
visit he was more than a little surprised to arrive at the
house of the Shaykh and be kept waiting a full half
hour in the birúní room.

In those days the homes of the upper class families
were comprised of two sections. The outer section was
called the 'birúní' where the guests were entertained
and where the men's reception room was found. The
inner section called the 'andarúní' was the private
living quarters of the family and where the ladies of
the household received their women relatives and
friends. The rooms opened onto the hayát, the
courtyard with a central pool surrounded by fruit
trees, flowers and shrubs.

Eventually the Shaykh, appearing distraught, entered from the andarúní, and greeted the somewhat
irritated Ibráhím. Apologizing he explained that his
daughter was quite ill. "She has shown no signs of recovery and has been given up on by the doctors treat-
ing her," lamented the Shaykh in a distressed tone.
"She is my only child," he added dejectedly, "I am
desperately worried and at my wits end to know what
to do".

Ibráhím comforted him with, "Do not worry, the matter can be resolved." Asking for and receiving paper, pen and ink he proceeded to write the name 'Abbás' in capital letters on the four corners of a sheet. Handing it to the Shaykh, he instructed him to soak the paper in a glass of water, and then have his daughter drink the water. The Shaykh, receptive to the younger man's directive, assured him he would. Then, with the two exchanging polite farewells, Ibráhím took his leave. In the meantime the girl's father faithfully carried out the instructions and the same day her fever broke; in a very short time she was well again.

Within a few days the mujtahid arrived at Ibráhím's home. Solemnly he informed Shaykh Najaf-'Alí of a fateful promise he had made to the Almighty that he would give his daughter in marriage to whichever physician would cure her. In a grave tone of commitment he said, "Since it was your son who provided the remedy which healed her, then my daughter shall be his."

Ibráhím's father was not unpleased to hear this for he knew that in all Burázján there was no young woman more beautiful or wealthy than she. With the two older men concurring, Ibráhím was approached, told the story of the girl's recovery and her father's vow; he agreed to the proposed marriage.

Several days later the two families had already begun preparations for the event but all ended abruptly because of a dream that Ibráhím had. In the dream a voice was heard to say, "Do not marry or you will become immersed in difficulty." This was repeated three times. Early next morning, with the words still

31

echoing in his mind, Ibráhím fled the town, heading for the port of Búshíhr by the Persian Gulf.

Distressed over his disappearance Ibráhím's father, along with the rest of his family, began a lengthy, intense but futile search for him. While everyone continued to wonder as to Ibráhím's whereabouts and why he had left, a merchant of Burázján, in Búshihr on business, spied Ibráhím and quickly discovered where he was staying. Aware of the family's plight, the merchant, without finishing his business, mounted his steed and rode back to Burázján with the news of Ibráhím's whereabouts.

Suspecting that Ibráhím's disappearance was related to the marriage plans, Shaykh Najaf 'Alí wrote to his son urging that if such was the case he should come home and making it clear that no one wanted to force him to go through with the marriage if he had changed his mind about it. It was a relieved Ibráhím who returned to Burázján soon after.

Ten

A Special Book

One night following his return Ibráhím experienced another dream; in it he saw a young man handing him a book and informing him that what the book contained would lead him to the end of his search. He soon forgot the dream but one day close to sunset while he was seated in the birúní section of the house there came a knock on the door. Customarily anyone who arrived at the entrance of the home of any of the ulamá (distinguished theologians) would find it open, and, having no need to knock, could enter without asking permission. Hearing the knock he arose, entered the long corridor between the house and the entrance door (the dálun) and asked who it was. A pleasant voice answered and Ibráhím, attracted by its warmth and charm, felt immediately drawn to the stranger to whom it belonged.

Opening the door he queried politely, "For whom are you looking?" In the dim evening light the stranger, standing a few steps back, replied, "For you, it is you I have come to see.".

With the visibility poor Ibráhím, wishing to see better, took a step closer. As he did he was able to see by the young man's appearance that he was newly arrived in Burázján. By means of further polite questioning Ibráhím learned that the stranger was from Shíráz, that he was travelling to Bushíhr but had come to Burázján to see him. So charmed was he by the bearing, speech and manner of his guest that it did not occur to Ibráhím to ask of the stranger his reason for wanting to see him. It was then, as Ibráhím appeared to have no more questions, that the young man, continuing in a friendly tone, posed one of his own. "Are you not Áqá Shaykh Muḥammad-Ibráhím?" "I am" said Ibráhím in acknowledgment. Convinced it was him the stranger had come to see, Ibráhím politely stepped to one side and, gesturing with open hands, invited the young man to enter the house, assuring him his horse would be put into the stable and his saddlebag brought in immediately.

When the two entered the house the stranger, having been offered an opportunity to wash and rest, was served tea and refreshments. Then began a fascinating conversation. Such was the enchanting effect of the stranger's words as he spoke with relaxed ease on a broad range of topics, that Ibráhím could not but be enamoured and entertained by the presence of the young man, filled with a sense of pleasure in his company and gratitude for his being there. At length, with the evening wearing on, the traveller accepted an invitation from Ibráhím to partake of dinner and stay the night.

Next morning at breakfast Ibráhím noticed there was a double lock on the stranger's saddlebag. Intrigued, he asked, "Friend, placing two locks on your saddle bag would suggest that it is filled with gold coins." "What I have there," the young man replied, "is more precious by far than gold." When Ibráhím followed politely with, "What is it that could be of such value?" The stranger, pausing to add gravity to his short answer, replied soberly but with a gentle smile on his lips and an angelic glint in his eye, "A book".

At that, Ibráhím's mounting curiosity gripped him with a sense of urgency. "May I see it?" he asked, straining to control an anticipation unlike any he had known before. "Of course", said the young man. He immediately opened the saddlebag, reached into it and slowly, with care, drew out the volume. Setting down the saddlebag he gripped the book in both his hands, raised it to his lips and, in a gesture which could only be reverent, he offered it to Ibráhím's waiting hands; it was a hand-written copy of the Kitáb-i-Íqán, (The Book of Certitude).[6]

As Ibráhím held the book the stranger told him he could peruse it for the next several hours because he intended to visit the Bázár (Persian market), but since he planned to leave in the afternoon, he would require that the book be returned by then. Ibráhím's entreaties to stay a few more days could not dissuade the young man from his firm intention to leave as planned. His host instructed the cook to prepare a good meal that could be placed in the visitor's saddlebag, as he was ready to leave.

Satisfied he had done all that propriety dictated, Ibráhím turned his attention to the book so graciously and fortuitously left in his possession for only the next few hours. It was as his right hand touched the front cover to open it that he suddenly remembered the dream in which he was handed a book by a young man and told that within its pages he would find that which his mind and heart desired to know. The experience of the next few hours was one that would, as its ramifications were to unfold, bring an abiding joy to his heart, but changes in him that would fill his family and friends with suspicion and dismay.

By one o'clock in the afternoon when his guest returned Ibráhím had finished the book. Never had such a world of Divine knowledge opened before him. A new radiance had dawned in his soul shedding within it a profound light and dispelling the misgivings that had overshadowed questions he had long pondered. Having thus imbibed so deeply of the Divine elixir his thirst but grew and his longing for more increased.

The two ate lunch together and finally, when the young man arose to leave, Ibráhím asked him if he might be kind enough to allow him to keep the book.

Aware of the subtle change in Ibráhím's demeanour and sensing the purity of his longing for the Word of God, he offered other material in lieu of the book, stating apologetically that it was his only asset. From a black cloth in which were wrapped a number of documents, he removed some Tablets and Verses revealed by Bahá'u'lláh, among them the Long Obligatory Prayer, the Tablet of Vision, the Tablet of 'Arz-i-Khá, (Khurásán) plus the Question and Answers Tablet, then handed them to Ibráhím, bid a gracious farewell, and departed.

A SPECIAL BOOK

Although Ibráhím did not know who had written the Kitáb-i-Íqán he was convinced beyond any doubt that the contents of it were truths Divinely revealed. Recognizing that what had been left him was of the same origin he set about memorizing, first the Long Obligatory Prayer, which he used every day, then gradually the remaining Tablets.

Eleven

Attempt on His Life

It was not long before observers resident in the area began noticing that since the traveller's visit a profound transformation had occurred in Ibráhím's condition and that there was a marked change in his talks and the views he expressed. Suspicions arose in their minds, at length convincing them that he had become a member of the heretical Bábí movement. Those individuals, who out of rivalry had borne a grudge towards Ibráhím, now fuelled their religious bigotry and fanaticism with a fresh measure of hatred and spite. Particular family relatives who thought Ibráhím's very existence brought shame and disgrace upon them and that he should be put away, conspired to choose from within the clan the one named Ismá'íl, known to all as the most vile, the most wicked, the most degraded and ignoble, to end Ibráhím's life.

Ismá'íl accepted the task. His plan was simple: to gain entry to Ibráhím's house, disguise his evil intent and at an opportune moment, stab him to death with a blade he would conceal in his cloak.

It was during Ramadán, the Muslim month of fasting, when on the chosen day, as the light of the late afternoon sun was waning, he entered the house and found Ibráhím seated in his room by the samovar of boiling water, drinking the tea he had just prepared.

Uninvited, the vile Ismá'íl, for whom Ibráhím had never any use, took a seated position near Ibráhím thinking he would await nightfall, commit his act and make his escape into the dark.

Aware of his malicious intent, Ibráhím said to him with steel in his voice, "What do you want? Why are you seated here?"

"I have come to break my fast and eat with you," was the lying reply.

The steel hardened and without hesitation Ibráhím spoke words that chilled Ismá'íl to his darkened core; "Go and eat in your own house," he ordered.

Shaking with fear and dismay, Ibráhím's would-be slayer arose and, without a word, departed.

On another occasion, with his evil intent rekindled and his miserable soul in the grip of fresh resolve, Ismá'íl once again entered Ibráhím's room and finding him seated, sat down himself. With first a contemptuous glance toward the unwelcome visitor and then in a voice that matched his piercing glare, Ibráhím turned and demanded, "What is your business here?"

There was a moment's pause before the reply.

"I have come to pay you a visit", came the words in a tone of feigned friendship. While Ibráhím remained silent his visitor sought to extend the charade just long enough to provide for him an opportunity to lunge at Ibráhím, plunge in the knife and make his cowardly escape.

The crude plan failed. When Ismá'íl leapt to his feet, as though reaching for a plate of dates on a shelf near his quarry and was about to draw forth the knife, his eyes met Ibráhím's and, as though held in a vice by them, he found himself powerless to go further. Confused, he nervously reached for a date, and then sitting back down could do nothing but begin eating it. Several more pathetic attempts resulted in a similar paralysis of will and with each failure his terror mounted.

Clearly aware of his intention and taking note of his state, Ibráhím challenged him saying, "Why are you rubbing your hands together? Why are you agitated?"

Ismá'íl, aware that the robe Ibráhím was wearing had been given to him by his dervish friend, 'Abdu'l Hamid, imagined that it was, by some mysterious power, causing him to be overwhelmed with fear, answered peevishly, "Can you not see I am cold, I am even shivering; let me borrow your robe to warm myself."

"You are unworthy to wear this; if you are cold get a blanket from the next room," was Ibráhím's stern response. Aware that the room was that of Ibráhím's mother, the very thought of whom intensified his fearful state, Ismá'íl suddenly got to his feet and fled the house, his terror pursuing him.

On another failed attempt by Ismá'íl, the mother of Ibráhím was even more directly involved. It occurred while Ibráhím was performing his Salavát, or evening prayer; as he assumed the sitting position he became aware of an inner voice urging him to get up and lock the door. The urgency so dominated his mind that finally he broke his prayer, secured the lock and returned to his prayerful position. Moments later he heard the sound of a knob turning and of pressure being applied to the locked door. This happened several times before he heard his mother's voice calling, "Who's there?" A voice from the other side of the door replied, "It is me, Ismá'íl."

"What do you want and why are you here?" snapped Ibráhím's mother, impatiently. Such a reply instantly stripped Ismá'íl of whatever vestiges of dark resolve he might have had; rather than reply a second time, his cowardice carried him into the darkness and he was gone. The voice of Ibráhím's mother could then be heard demanding angrily of the servant why the front door had not been locked.

Presently his mother appeared in Ibráhím's room and began to admonish him. She was fearfully aware of the danger Ibráhím had placed himself in by the recent changes in his demeanour, the inflammatory things he had been saying and that because of this, many were convinced that he should be killed.

"For the sake of God," she pleaded, "stop saying such things and making more enemies. You must protect yourself. The ulamá and family members have said they will kill you to prevent you disgracing them further. It is very difficult for your father; he agreed with them that you merit such treatment but because he has always loved you he keeps silence."

That night Ibráhím weighed thoughtfully what his mother had said and, considering it in the light of recent experience, knew that it was time to leave

Burázján. Besides, within him was a growing desire to know the historical roots of his newfound Faith. Aware that the centre of activities of the Faith was in the Holy Land and knowing it would not be prudent to ask his father for funds to journey there, he decided to tell his father that he wished to complete his research and learning and that he would therefore need to travel, once again, to Atabát-i-Álíat in Iráq, the vicinity of the Holy Shrines of Islám's Shi'ah sect. His father agreed and the funds were forthcoming.

Twelve

In Search of the Beloved

Because his brother, Shaykh Muḥammad-Ḥusayn was residing in Najaf, one of the cities in the area, Ibrahim decided to journey there first. His brother welcomed him and, once settled, Ibráhím wasted no time initiating a study class. After an introductory period of discourse he began to explain the poetic verses of the Ḥájí Mullá Hádí and to combine their philosophical content with the Divine teachings in his possession, limited as they were. By this means a fresh lustre was added to the words he delivered, a development, however, which did not go unnoticed by his brother.

Although Ibráhím's eyes yearned to behold, and his heart to be united with his Lord, he waited patiently, believing that some indication of the direction his quest should carry him would sooner or later be made known. Convinced it would be unwise to make overt inquiries, he waited in a state of complete resignation and trust that the information he needed would, at the right time, be disclosed to him, perchance in the course of a conversation. His patience was at length rewarded, for at last he learned he must go to 'Akká.

43

Pondering his forthcoming journey, it seemed best that he should, for safety's sake, join a caravan destined for Meccá and at a certain point break off from it in the direction of 'Akká. With this in mind he made arrangements to depart, at the beginning of the winter, with a caravan bound for Hijáz.

When the time came for his departure and on the morning he was to leave, he roused his brother and broke the news of his immanent journey.

"What is your destination?" queried his brother. "Akká", said Ibráhím. His brother paused, that name causing a subtle expression to creep into his eyes. "Then", said his brother, confirming what for some time he had suspected, "all those new notions and phrases you were incorporating into your discourses came from the Bábís?" When Ibráhím answered in the affirmative his brother concluded, "Then, you are a Bábí!" "No", was Ibráhím's reply, "I am a Bahá'í." Another pause followed while his brother thoughtfully considered the obvious consequence to himself and his family of the words he was hearing.

With a note of alarm in his voice Shaykh Husayn asked, "What should I say to our father?"

It was Ibráhím who now paused, knowing full well what his father's reaction would be upon hearing that his son was now a 'Bábí'.

"Tell our father," he said, "that I have gone, and shall not be returning."

Recovering; and with astute presence of mind his brother asked, "Since this separation will be permanent, would you then leave your seal and personal documents in my trust?"

So little concerned was Ibráhím with worldly possessions and so preoccupied was he with thoughts of
his journey to 'Akká, that he handed his things to his
brother, failing to realize that his brother intended to
use Ibráhím's seal in order to prepare a letter of agreement for the transfer of Ibráhím's considerable inheritance, to himself.

As the thought of needing money crossed his mind
Ibráhím was moved to ask his brother for some and
was given the equivalent of two or three Tumáns (Persian currency). With that plus a meagre supply of food
and his feet clad only in slippers, he bade farewell to
his brother, left Najaf on foot and joined one of the
several caravans destined for Meccá.

People tend to form opinions about those in whose
company they are journeying; some who do, especially
if their opinions are negative, are not reticent about
making them known. Ibráhím's fellow travellers, judg-
ing him by his appearance, believed he was a hajj
dealer, a person whom others would pay to make a
pilgrimage on their behalf. Having a low regard for
such people, seeing them as vile, inferior and con-
temptible because they would choose to walk rather
than rent a camel, they heaped their scorn and abuse
on Ibráhím.

For the duration of his journey with the caravan the
weather was mild enabling the caravan to travel by day
and stop at night to rest. At night when the travellers
would lodge at a caravanserai he would enter one of
the Kijávíhs to sleep.

Most travellers in that time rode on horses, camels
or mules. A Kijávíh, 'that which hangs crooked', is

made of two large, open boxes or panniers, roped together and placed, hanging on a slant, on either side over the back of a mule. This allowed for one passenger to sit inside each pannier gravitating towards the centre. If one passenger's weight was lighter the muleteer would have to add some heavy objects or stones to even the weight of both sides.

Scarcely could one have travelled more simply than Ibráhím chose to. Besides the sparse quantity of food with him, he carried only a teapot and a small glass container wrapped in a coarse sac. On his feet he wore only slippers and because they were soon in shreds the rigours of walking barefoot took their toll. Eventually, he was able to replace the torn slippers with a pair of gíveh (cotton hand-crocheted summer shoes) he had purchased in one of the villages along the way.

One evening of the journey Ibráhím became involved in a unique experience he could never have anticipated. The caravan had halted at an Inn; to rest their animals the camel owners had made the decision to remain there for two nights. On the morning after the first night Ibráhím noticed a village not far ahead and set out for it hopeful that he would be able to purchase some sugar and tea. Finding it to be larger than it first appeared he made his way into it and entered an alleyway in search of a shop where he could make his purchases. Suddenly he grew apprehensive, startled by the sight of a man rushing towards him. The man, who, as it turned out, was actually the 'kadkhudá', (the village chief) stopped a short distance from him and began to bow. Excitedly he exclaimed, "You are an angel!"

Ibráhím, still somewhat afraid, stared in amazement, hoping for an explanation.

"Last night you appeared to me in a dream looking exactly as you do now! Please come!" he entreated, gesturing broadly with his hand. "Come with me to my house, please!"

So far this was not enough to convince Ibráhím. Sensing Ibráhím's misgivings, the man heaved a sigh then explained, anxiously, "I have a daughter who is choking because of a leech that has been lodged in her throat these past four days. She is in pain and bleeding and I am at my wits end; no one has been able to remove it. Last night, desperate, I sobbed and called out to God. Finally I slept but in a dream I saw *you!*" The man went on, "It was clear to me you would be the one to save my daughter; and when I saw you on the street I could not believe my eyes; you are here! I beseech you then, come to my house. Please!"

Ibráhím reluctantly agreed and followed the man. As they walked his thoughts turned upon the peculiar incident just related to him. Having not the slightest idea what it was he might do to help the child, he turned his heart to God and silently asked for guidance. Then suddenly he remembered Abdul-Ḥamíd, the mystic in the Haft-Tan of S͟híráz who taught him that, by writing the name 'Abbás in ink in the quadrants of a piece of paper and soaking the ink out with water, then having the sufferer drink the water, recovery would take place. The procedure had worked for the mujtahid's daughter in Burázján the one time he prescribed it; why should he not try it again? Yes, why not!

As they entered the chief's home Ibráhím turned to him and said, with absolute confidence, "What I instruct you to do, do it and your daughter will get well. But this prescription is conditional upon providing me with a place to sleep, I need rest."

The chief expressed his warm-hearted willingness whereupon Ibráhím explained the procedure then asked for the paper, ink and pen and, when it was given him, promptly wrote the benediction and handed it to the girl's father. In turn the grateful father prepared some bedding in the living room then left with the inscribed paper. The tired Ibráhím was soon asleep.

Within minutes his instructions were scrupulously carried out by his anxious host who carefully obtained the benediction water, poured it slowly into the mouth of his suffering daughter and obliged her to swallow it. The girl soon began coughing and in a matter of seconds the leach was propelled from her throat.

News of this remarkable restoration to well being could not be contained within the household and, although night had fallen, word of it spread to every inhabitant of the village. By morning crowds of people had surrounded the house. When Ibráhím awoke and opened his eyes, it was to see the room in which he had slept full of villagers. All had been standing quietly, waiting for the moment he would open his eyes. Some were crippled, some blind, some injured and the rest sick; each was hopeful that Ibráhím would heed their as yet unspoken request to be healed. As he was registering his surprise he also noticed that the room had warmed considerably. Then he caught sight of the chief gesturing to the silent crowd, his finger to his lips, hoping they would avoid making noises that would awaken his guest.

When Ibráhím finally gathered his thoughts and arose from the place where he had slept, the roomful of desperate souls closed in upon him, all voicing at the same time an urgent personal request for Ibráhím to work his healing power and make them whole. Each had brought a gift for the healer, whose presence among them had suddenly filled their lives with hope.

Noticing it was still dark outside, Ibráhím was reminded that his caravan was to leave at dawn, so in haste he wrote a few prescription 'notes' and, apologizing that he had to leave, entrusted the pieces of paper to the chief explaining that should he stay longer he would surely miss the caravan. Quickly he chose a few of the gifts and, placing them into his sack, left hurriedly, managing to rejoin the caravan just as it was about to leave.

Within a few more days of travel the caravan reached a crossroad and there, separating himself from it, he set off in the direction of Beirut.

Thirteen

First Encounter With a Bahá'í

Many days later, on foot, fatigued and exhausted he reached the city where, without delay and according to the instructions given him in Najaf, he set about to find a Bahá'í merchant who was residing there, one Áqá Muḥammad- Muṣṭafáy-i- Baghdádí.

This firm, steadfast and well-informed believer, who was also a poet and literary man, had served Bahá'u'lláh as a young man in Baghdád and accompanied Him on his exile to Constantinople. He had completely dedicated his life to serving the Faith. It was through him that messages and letters from the believers from all parts were sent to 'Abdu'l-Bahá. Tablets revealed by Him in reply were in turn received by Áqá Muṣṭafá and dispatched all over the world. Another very important function he was appointed to perform was to guide and assist the travellers and pilgrims in order to protect them from the Covenant-breakers who were intent upon casting doubt and scepticism among the believers. The Baghdádí home in Beirut was well known to the Bahá'ís everywhere for its warmth and for the loving hospitality showered upon the stream of visitors who entered it, whether en route to, or returning from 'Akká.

Áqá Muḥammad-Muṣṭafá had three sons, all staunch and firm in the Covenant. One of them, well known to the North American Bahá'ís, was Dr. Ziá Bagdadi, who practiced medicine in Chicago and rendered outstanding service as a great Bahá'í teacher in the United States.

Finding the Baghdádí home and, upon meeting Áqá Muṣṭafá, Ibráhím introduced himself then gave an account of his story and his decision to reach Akká in hopes of attaining the presence of his Lord. Áqá Muṣṭafá spoke comforting words of welcome and warmly invited the pilgrim into his house.

Ibráhím spent only long enough in Beirut to refresh himself and gain a little strength before setting off for 'Akká. During that stay his Bahá'í friend recounted to him facts dealing with the rebellion of 'Abdul-Bahá's half brother Mírzá Muḥammad-'Alí (whose rebellion, by then, had reached its peak) and the activities of the Covenant-breakers.[7] After giving some money to Ibráhím for the remainder of his journey he described to him precautions he must take and gave instructions regarding the correct route he should follow to reach 'Akká. He emphasized that upon his arrival he should proceed directly to the musáfir khánih (the upper rooms of a caravanserai) and avoid all other places; the Covenant breakers were lurking about to ambush newly arrived pilgrims to the Holy Land with the ruse of a friendly greeting but the dark purpose of casting into their minds the seeds of doubt and scepticism.

Muḥammad-Ibráhím arrived at the prison city of 'Akká in the year 1320 AH (1903). The years prior to that (1901-1902) had brought about distress, fresh trials, deep sorrow and anguish for 'Abdu'l-Bahá and His followers, originating, as ever, from the rash and wicked plotting of His seditious half brother, Mírzá Muḥammad-'Alí as well as other family members. They had resolved to bring to an end the work started by'Abdu'l-Bahá on the construction of the shrine of the Báb, (the Prophet Herald of the Bahá'í Faith) during the early months of the 20th Century's opening year. Viewed as a great chance to capture the attention and kindle the anger of Sultán 'Abdu'l Ḥamid, ruler of the Ottoman Empire, these violators of the Covenant of Bahá'u'lláh accused 'Abdu'l-Bahá of undertaking to erect a fortress half way up Mount Carmel on a site facing the Bay of Haifa and beyond, the blue Mediterranean. Because of these lying provocations, a decree of the Sultán arrived confining 'Abdu'l-Bahá to within the city limits of 'Akká and as a result, pilgrimages were halted. Towards the end of 1902, however, restrictions were such that 'Abdu'l-Bahá was again able to permit pilgrims from east and west to come to the Holy Land and attain His presence.

It was fortuitous that it had taken Ibráhím two years from the time of his arrival in Najaf until he was finally shown his destination, the direction in which he must travel, the place he must reach in order to meet the Head of his new-found Faith. For during that time there had been restrictions under which no pilgrims could visit. Yet by the time of his arrival the restrictions had eased, making it considerably less difficult for pilgrims in general.

Fourteen

Threshold of Attainment

Having travelled a few months on foot Ibráhím, on a warm afternoon early in the summer of 1903 finally, through its iron gate, entered the City of 'Akká. It was a thrilling thing for him to find himself in that ancient prison town walking through its dark winding lanes with their high forbidding walls of plaster and stone, and to realize that somewhere amongst its inhabitants was the object of his quest, the goal and purpose of his journey, a journey he had begun not months but years before. This realization filled his heart with joy and fanned the flame of his mounting anticipation.

Following the instructions given him Ibráhím began his search for the caravanserai but was not prepared for what he was soon to see. Making his way, on directions from a passer-by, through a twisted maze of carved narrow streets, he rounded a corner and found himself some distance behind a group of men walking ahead of him. His soul leapt with excitement; even from behind he knew the man leading the group to be one of the two holy personages he, in <u>Kh</u>urásán, had seen in a vision standing before the Majestic Throne of God.

Feeling it would be an act of disrespect to attempt to enter His presence by approaching Him from behind, and believing that later, at the appropriate time, he would be granted such a privilege, Ibráhím chose rather to continue his search for the caravanserai called Khán-i-Omrán (the Production Inn).

It was a place where daily, in its central courtyard, a wide variety of grains, citrus and other fruits were loaded and unloaded to or from the backs of camels, mules and horses. It was a dirty and smelly place full of flies and filth and Arabs plying their merchandise. The lower level rooms around the courtyard were used to lodge the drivers while the rooms of the upper part, off balconies facing the courtyard, had been rented for the use of the Bahá'ís. On the east side there was a large room that faced the sea and was occupied by the pilgrims and next to it was the kitchen. On the west side there were a few small rooms that housed the resident believers such as Hájí Mírzá Haydar-'Alí, "the angel of Carmel", Jináb-i-Mishkín Qalam, the well known calligrapher, and Jináb-i-Zaynu'l-Muqarrabín, once the high priest of Isfahán who had suffered many hardships and years of imprisonment as a Bahá'í and who, in his beautiful and skilled handwriting, had inscribed a great many Tablets of Bahá'u'lláh. Detached from all worldly pleasures and material ease and comfort, their only desire was to be near their Master, attain His presence, listen to His voice and utterance, partake of His grace and favours and, content with little nourishment and meagre living conditions,

55

endeavour to serve Him to the best of their abilities. They slept on the floor on light mattresses or pads which they rolled up in the daytime and placed, along with their rolled up belongings, by one of the walls of the room thus allowing space for people to sit, pray, eat and visit.

The cook was a dignified, submissive and agile man by the name of Áqá Muḥammad-Ḥassan-i-Khádim, who not only prepared everyone's meals singlehandedly, but also cleaned the rooms, laundered the clothes, purchased the food, washed dishes and served everyone tea. The food he prepared was simple and everyone, rich or poor, ate the same thing. Breakfast included two small glasses of sweet tea and some whole wheat bread; for lunch there was always a big pot of ábgousht, the Persian equivalent of stew, and some sour bread. Everyone was happy and content, not interested in outward pleasures but much attracted to and enamoured of their Lord. Often in order to show affability and to encourage the pilgrims the Master would come to visit them, eat the same food, check on things in the kitchen and give the cook some instructions.

At the top of the stairs was the entrance to the balcony and there, located where everyone removed their shoes, was a cage hanging with a parrot inside it. Whenever 'Abdu'l-Bahá entered, the parrot greeted him with, "Alláh'u'Abhá!" (God is the Most Glorious!). Its voice was so loud and clear that it could be heard from a considerable distance and, when 'Abdu'l-Bahá would answer with "Alláh'u'Abhá!", sometimes the parrot would say, "Marhabá!" (Well done!).

Eventually Ibráhím found the building. Pausing momentarily in front of it, he looked about but saw no one in the vicinity. Just then a figure approached him from the late afternoon shadows and cordially introduced himself as Áqá Najaf-'Alí, the gatekeeper, but added, with a slight note of regret, "Only a few short minutes ago, my companions locked up the entrance to the quarters and left." After a brief moment of thought he then said, "Please, rest yourself while I go to pick up the keys", then invited Ibráhím to wait for him in the adjoining coffee house.

Ibráhím, suspicious because of the warnings he had received from Áqá Muṣṭafá and wary that the man might be a Covenant-breaker who planned to trick him into a meeting with his leader, spoke to him in a stern voice laced with anger, "I have not come here to spend my time in a coffee house." Then turning immediately toward the stairs he proceeded to the caravanserai's upper level but found the door locked.

Áqá Najaf-'Alí, who had followed him up the stairs, stopped as Ibráhím turned to face him and, gesturing openly with his hands, the gatekeeper spoke amicably, "You are absolutely right, I agree with you; but please, the coffee house is also a place of 'Abdu'l-Bahá's, it is my most sincere wish that you make yourself comfortable there while I go to His Holiness and tell him you have arrived."

Ibráhím, feeling somewhat assured, finally agreed and descended to a door at the building's ground level, making his way into the coffee house as Najaf-'Alí hurried off to tell the Master.

He arrived at 'Abdu'l-Bahá's dwelling to find that some prominent Bahá'í teachers, namely, Jináb-i-Doctor Yúnis Afrou<u>kh</u>tih, Ḥájí 'Abdu'l Ḥassan Amín, Mi<u>sh</u>kin Qalam, Ḥájí Múnis, and Ḥájí Mírzá Ḥaydar-'Alí, were there along with several others, enjoying the honour of being present with the Master. Upon hearing Najaf-'Alí relate his story of the encounter with, "a nervous á<u>kh</u>und", (a mullá or Muslim theologian), the gathering grew momentarily fearful that Ibráhím might well have been sent on the instigation of the Covenant-breakers to carry out a spy mission for the ulamá.

But 'Abdu'l-Bahá, upon hearing of the visitor's arrival, turned to Ḥájí Mírzá Ḥaydar-'Alí[8] and said, "Go now to our dearly esteemed guest, take care of him, entertain him and attend to his needs; tomorrow morning I will send for him."

Given the suspicions, which had understandably arisen in their minds, all were astonished at hearing this and even then, their fears, though reduced, were not entirely put to rest.

Ibráhím was comfortably seated in the coffee house, awaiting the return of the gatekeeper when presently in he came, accompanied by an old man with a hunched back; it was Ḥájí Mírzá Ḥaydar-'Alí. While Najaf-'Alí went to unlock the second level door, Mírzá Ḥaydar-'Alí approached Ibráhím and initiated the exchange of courteous greetings and salutations before sitting down beside him. Politely, he asked Ibráhím where he had come from. Ibráhím replied, "Najaf". A series of questions from Mírzá Ḥaydar-'Alí ensued, delivered somewhat abruptly but nevertheless with genuine politeness. Ibráhím's answers were equally abrupt and in a tone which barely disguised the fact that with each question his cast of mind grew increasingly more offended. "Where are you from?" "Shíráz." "What is your religion?" "I am a Bahá'í." "And who is your teacher?" "No one!" "Who is your acquaintance?" "Nobody!" "On whose behalf are you here?" " My own." "Have you come on foot or did you ride?" "I walked." "And why have you come?" "To see my Lord," was Ibráhím's final and somewhat exasperated reply.

The interrogation, as Mírzá Ḥaydar-'Alí soon realized, was offering him not the slightest clue as to the identity of the newcomer. Rather, it increased his perplexity. Knowing that further questions would prove just as futile he arose, politely invited Ibráhím to follow him, then led him to the lodgings upstairs.

By this time other Bahá'ís had arrived and taken note of the "ákhund" with his hair long, dusty and dishevelled and his beard unkempt. Although they were unable to free themselves from the shadowy misgivings lodged in their minds, one thing was certain, they could not allow themselves to be overtly rude or speak to him disrespectfully. Had not the Master, before the assembled friends, instructed them to entertain this visitor as His newly arrived guest and to show him the most courteous regard? Eventually, with their suspicions still lingering, they all left. Ibráhím welcomed the opportunity of preparing himself for some much needed rest and was soon ready to retire for the night.

Fifteen

In the Presence of the Master

Next morning Ḥájí Mírzá Ḥaydar-'Alí dutifully arrived with a few others, bringing fresh clean clothes for the guest. The clothing included head attire in the form of a fez and the white cloth that wraps around it. Ibráhím was directed to where he could go and bathe himself. When he returned, wearing the supplied clothing, Ḥájí Mírzá Ḥaydar-'Alí asked him in a friendly manner to remain at the house while they went to obtain permission for him to gain the presence of 'Abdu'l-Bahá. A short while later Áqá Najaf-'Alí returned for Ibráhím and together they set off for the house of 'Abdu'l-Bahá.

The house to which Ibráhím was taken to meet 'Abdu'l-Bahá was known as the former home of Abdu'lláh Páshá. The house had a large courtyard with a pool, flowering plants and tall trees. On one side of it there were stairs leading up and, upon reaching the top, one entered a kafshkan, a little hallway where visitors removed their shoes. On the right hand side, one step up, was 'Abdu'l-Bahá's day reception room with windows facing the sea.

In recent years this house was purchased by the Bahá'í World Centre and refurnished under the very able direction of Amatu'l-Bahá Rúhíyyih Khánum, wife of the Guardian of the Bahá'í Faith, and elevated by him to the rank of Hand of the Cause of God.[9] The house, as a result of the refurnishing, now appears the same as it had been in the time of 'Abdu'l-Bahá. It was officially opened for the Bahá'ís to visit on the occasion of the Sixth International Convention held in April of 1988 in Haifa, Israel. At that time delegates to the Convention had the privilege of being taken to 'Akká to visit the various rooms of the house, including the room in which the beloved Guardian, Shoghi Effendi, was born, March 1st, 1897. The writer had the bounty of being a delegate to that Convention and it was a profoundly moving experience for her as she entered the very room, 'Abdu'l-Bahá's day reception room, where so many years before, her grand-father had entered and attained the presence of his beloved Master.

Half an hour before Ibráhím arrived with Áqá Najaf-'Alí, two visitors from the city had come to see 'Abdu'l-Bahá, one was the Mufti of 'Akká, the other, one of the ulamá (or Muslim theologians) of the city, who had a question for the Master concerning the Caliphate[10]. As Ibráhím entered the room the Master was speaking, using statements from the Qur'án to demonstrate the rectitude and competence of the, "Commander of the Faithful", the Imám 'Alí, in relation to the matter of the Caliphate. It is important to mention that the inhabitants of Akká belonged to the Sunní sect of Islam which do not accept the Imám 'Alí as the successor to the Prophet Muḥammad.

While Ibráhím awaited his opportunity to speak a word of greeting his eyes scanned the room. He noticed that, of the twelve chairs placed around, only the one to the immediate right of 'Abdu'l-Bahá (the seat of honour) was unoccupied. When 'Abdu'l-Bahá's voice paused in momentary silence, Ibráhím, knowing nothing of customary formalities or the commonly practiced local greetings, spoke one he knew to be widely accepted, "Salám'un-Aleikum", ("Peace be with you.")

The Master's eyes turned towards him and smiling, He spoke most warmly in a tone that immediately infused Ibráhím with a great feeling of happiness, "Marhabá! Marhabá! (Welcome! Welcome!) You have journeyed a great distance; Bismil-lláh!" Gesturing with open hands, in a most gracious and loving manner towards the chair beside Him, He then said, "Please, come and be seated".

The tone and the words he heard embraced Ibráhím's heart. In that sun-filled moment all the fatigue from the toil of the long journey left him and his soul was flooded with a joy and exhilaration such as he had never before known. He obediently seated himself beside 'Abdu'l-Bahá, who then returned to His dissertation on the rank of the Imám 'Alí.

Then a strange thing happened. In the midst of the stream of the Master's words Ibráhím found himself audibly and involuntarily repeating a verse of the Qur'án relating to the subject. There was a brief moment of silence in which all present sat in wide-

63

eyed wonderment, for what they had just heard could well have been construed by some as impertinence and disrespect. Their attention was on the Master; they saw Him turn His face towards Ibráhím who, with head bent and eyes downcast, did not know what to feel about what had just escaped from his lips. He alone did not see the face of ʻAbdu'l-Bahá smiling broadly. In the next instant the Master gave hearty utterance to words which would determine how believers were to henceforth regard this "ákhund".

"Yes of course, Jináb-i-Fádil! That is correct!" exclaimed ʻAbdu'l-Bahá. "These gentlemen", He said, "have not really read the Qur'án nor do they have a true knowledge of the Qur'ánic verses..." and proceeded to shower Ibráhím with glowing praise.

Such a bestowal of favour by the Master dispelled, forever, suspicions the others may have entertained concerning the newcomer's identity. In their attempts to determine it, some had imagined him a simple talabá (student of theology), others, an ordinary ákhund. With the title, "Fádil" (Learned), having been given him only moments before by their wise and unerring Master, they now realized that the new arrival in their midst was of such learning and erudition as to be recognized by a title of distinction never before bestowed by the Master upon a follower of the new Faith.

The writer wishes to explain that although there have been several eminent Baháʼís who, during the early history of the Faith, were known by the name Fádil, such as Jináb-i-Áqá Muhammad Fádil-i-Qáʼiní and Jináb-i-Fádil-i-Mázandarání, the name Fádil had not been bestowed upon them by a Central Figure of the Faith. In the case of the well-known Fádil-i-Qá'ini, he was honoured with the title of Nabil-i-Akbar from the tongue of Bahá'u'lláh Himself and was refered to by 'Abdu'l-Bahá as a Hand of the Cause.

As each member of the gathering turned over in his mind what he had just witnessed, 'Abdu'l-Bahá resumed His discourse. Upon concluding, He turned to Jináb-i-Fádil and said to him with kindness and loving consideration, "You are very tired, please go back to the caravanserai and rest". Then, turning to Ḥájí Mírzá Ḥaydar-'Alí he said, "I am entrusting our guest to your care. Fiamán'el-lláh!"(Go in God's safety!).

With that, all the believers rose and slowly departed the room. Once outside the house there were many cordial attempts to shake hands with Fádil, embrace him and, as was customary, place a kiss on both his cheeks. Fádil, however, reliving his uneasiness and the offence he had taken over the suspicious interrogations of the previous night, addressed them in a tone decidedly harsh and with words that made it clear he did not want to be kissed.

Sixteen

Encouragement of 'Abdu'l-Bahá

An incident further indicating 'Abdu'l-Bahá's special regard for Fádil occurred next morning after Fádil, in the company of a group of believers, arrived in the presence of the Master. With the Master was a noted Bahá'í physician, Dr. Yunís Khán-i- Afroukhtih. 'Abdu'l-Bahá turned to him and remarked in a spiritually playful way, "Fádil was introduced to the Faith by us; let us now see the difference between one that we have taught and one taught by yourself". In deference, the amiable doctor humbly observed, "Your Honour, whatever we deliver is like a copper coin, what you deliver is 'gawhar-i-shab chirágh' (a radiant gem)".

Fádil's sojourn in 'Akká lasted four months and during that time 'Abdu'l-Bahá advised the friends repeatedly that they should take advantage of Fádil's presence among them by seeking to benefit from his knowledge. Acting on the Master's advice they besought Fádil to initiate evening classes for them. Fádil was willing and classes began in the Pilgrim House but much to his dismay Fádil realized early on that his

'Abdu'l-Bahá

mystical teaching was over their heads. As a new member of the Bahá'í Community and having a great desire to be of service, this perplexed him to the point of depression. He suspended the classes.

Soon after this 'Abdu'l-Bahá asked the believers how the evenings at the Pilgrim House were going? Somewhat ashamed of the fact that Fádil had been silent the past several nights and of the reason why, no one offered to answer. As the believers were taking leave of His presence the Master asked Fádil to remain, then to accompany Him on a walk outdoors. As they walked 'Abdu'l-Bahá related the story of a sage who had been jailed and found himself thrust into the company of an ignorant man. The sage was soon complaining to the king that any punishment, calamity or affliction the king could choose to visit upon him would not be worse than forcing him to keep company with the ignorant man.

The Master continued to remove the pain Fádil was suffering, assuring him that he should not allow the failure of the friends to grasp the abstruse terms and deep meanings of spiritual knowledge he had been attempting to impart, cause him offence. With kind and loving words, which also included an instructive poem, the Master encouraged him and helped him to appreciate the idea that when teaching children, the language of a child should be used. These counsels and exhortations, given Fádil with such loving and tender affection by 'Abdu'l-Bahá, not only gave him fresh enthusiasm to resume the classes he had been giving, they remained a constant source of encourage-

ment to him in his teaching efforts throughout the
rest of his life.

Seventeen

Secret Thoughts Made Known

There were many occasions during his sojourn in 'Akká that Fádil was present when 'Abdu'l-Bahá spoke to a gathering of friends. On one such occasion there were a great number of visitors in attendance when the thought occurred to Fádil that if he could only meet with Mírzá Muḥammad-'Alí (Qusn-i-Akbar, the Greater Branch, who was 'Abdu'l-Bahá's half brother and rebelled against Him) he could admonish and warn him and perchance awaken him to his folly. In that very instant, with the room crowded, 'Abdu'l-Bahá interrupted His talk, looked toward Fádil and, in what struck Fádil as a firm voice but tinged with sorrow and resignation, recited a poem in Arabic; the writer's translation of it follows:

"Grasp thou what thou beholdest,
Forsake thou what thou hast heard.
Before the sun's radiance,
Saturn doth not suffice thee."

'Abdu'l-Bahá then followed with these words: "After the ascension of the Blessed Countenance

71

(Bahá'u'lláh) I called my brother here and in our meeting I said we have no other desire but to exalt and to serve the blessed Cause of the Ancient Beauty so let us be united. We would conquer the East and you the West; We would encourage the friends in the Orient and you the friends in the Occident. We did our utmost to counsel him, showering him with love and affection. At one point We even wept, beseeching him and appealing to him not to allow the Cause to perish by breaking the Covenant and causing discord and dissension. It all had no effect whatsoever on him."

The Master's whole aspect had changed; sadness and grief covered His blessed countenance. Those present looked on in amazement while their hearts wondered at why the Centre of the Covenant had made mention of the Chief of Rebellion. But Fádil understood why and at once abandoned the notion he had entertained, knowing that 'Abdu'l-Bahá, through His innate power, was aware of his thoughts and had conveyed to him His response.

Witnessing one's secret thoughts voiced aloud by 'Abdu'l-Bahá was not uncommon among those who knew Him and spent time in His presence. Aware of 'Abdu'l-Bahá's spiritual perception, Fádil grew to understand that he never had to convey orally any wish to the Master. His Lord, by virtue of His innate power, knew Fádil's pure longings and would respond.

There was a time during his stay in 'Akká, when Fádil had been preoccupied with the fate of his own father, a man who bore such hatred for the Bahá'ís that, when he learned of his son's involvement in the Faith, had issued a denial of Ibráhím as his son, swore never to mention his name again and took steps to cut him off from his considerable inheritance. One day as Fádil's thoughts were revolving around his father it occurred to him that he might, on his father's behalf, ask 'Abdu'l-Bahá's pardon and forgiveness. Next day when he was seated before the Master an amazing thing took place that relieved Fádil's anxiety and bathed his spirit in warm assurances. 'Abdu'l-Bahá, whose face was turned toward the window overlooking the sea, spoke these words, "Jináb-i-Fádil, because of your recognition and belief in the Cause of God, many souls will be drowned in the ocean of God's forgiveness and pardon".

Eighteen

Nearing Departure

Eventually the time came for Fádil to take his leave. During the four months of his stay in 'Akká he had seen wonders, witnessed extraordinary things, and heard awe-inspiring stories which astounded him. What impacted his soul most forcibly and gave him such strength of conviction that he would dedicate all the remaining days of his life to the service of his Lord, was his close association with 'Abdu'l-Bahá on an almost daily basis. Witnessing His spiritual radiance, His meekness, His selflessness and His overflowing generosity, partaking of His Divine knowledge and wisdom and feeling that superhuman power pulsating in His creative words and utterances galvanized his soul's resolve. This would sustain him all his days despite the suffering he would endure over his father's rejection of him for joining the Bahá'í Faith and the grief he would bear realizing he would never see his mother again in this world.

It will be of interest to note here that Dr. Yunís Khán-i- Afroukhtih, who spent nine years (1900-1909) in 'Akká in the service of the Master as one of His devoted secretaries, makes reference in his memoirs to

seven different glances of 'Abdu'l-Bahá and explains
how each according to its nature would release
mysterious forces when directed towards a believer
who had attained His presence. He mentions one
which, above all, instantly bestowed true knowledge
and wisdom upon the person to whom it was directed.
Dr.Yunís Khán affirms that he himself had seen two
men who were attracted by such a glance and became
recipients of divine knowledge, "One," he says, "was
Fádil-i-Shírází and the other one was Shaykh 'Alí-
Akbar-i-Quchání"(a prominent Bahá'í martyr).

Two days before his departure, Fádil found himself
with several things weighing on his mind, some having
to do with his future, what shape it would take, what
course he would follow and the sorts of things he
should do? He also wondered over whether or not his
practice of rigorous self-discipline and the ascetic life,
his acquisition of knowledge and his painstaking
search after truth had been pleasing and acceptable to
the Master. But what stirred the desire of his heart
most fervently was the wish that 'Abdu'l-Bahá would
reveal a Tablet for him in His own handwriting.

By late afternoon on the day he was to leave 'Akká,
Fádil arrived at the house of 'Abdu'lláh-Páshá and, as
he entered the room in which a great number of believers were being addressed by the Master, noticed
that His hand was writing something on a piece of
paper. As the Master spoke His pen moved; He was
simultaneously uttering words of advice and exhorta-
tion to the attentive crowd while inscribing a message
on the piece of paper. Continuing to speak He finished writing then folded the Tablet and, placing it in

an envelope, beckoned to Ḥájí Mírzá Ḥaydar-'Alí who was sitting next to Fádil. Mírzá Ḥaydar-'Alí arose, went forward and 'Abdu'l-Bahá, as he handed him the envelope, spoke in undertones directly to him. Upon returning to his seat he explained to Fádil that the envelope was addressed to him and contained a Tablet revealed for him by the Master, adding words that surprised Fádil, "I will send it to you".

Sometime later the meeting ended. When the crowd had all left, the Master approached Fádil, put His hand gently on his shoulder and said, "Jináb-i-Fádil, you may ask for whatever you want." Fádil responded humbly and from his heart, "I wish only health and strength for you my Lord, and seek but to carry out your will and instructions". "Marhabá!"(Well done!) was the Master's response.

Nineteen

Final Words

It was now time for final instructions regarding the specific route Fádil should take on his return journey to Írán. After giving him 19 English pounds 'Abdu'l-Bahá counselled him that it was not advisable to go back the same way he had come, that is, via Najaf and Shíráz, for his identity as a Bahá'í was now known. Rather he should journey by way of Iṣtanbul and through Bádkubih in order to reach Rasht, the capital city of Guilán Province in Northern Írán. While traveling he should be circumspect and mention the Faith to no one.

During the course of his final words with Fádil the Master indicated that Fádil would no longer have need of what he had been carrying. Fádil knew immediately that 'Abdu'l-Bahá was referring to the elixer-powder and resolved, then and there, to commit it to the sea at the outset of his journey. (This is a fact Jináb-i-Fádil would have shared with no one but his immediate family. It was one of many instances in Fádil's life related to the author by her mother, the daughter of Jináb-i-Fádil). Finally, informing Fádil that he would receive instructions from Him in Rasht, the Master

77

embraced his disciple lovingly, and said, "Fiamán'el-lláh!" (Go in God's safety and protection).

On his final return to the caravanserai Fádil was longing to know the contents of the Tablet destined for him but not to be in his possession until some time later. He asked Mírzá Ḥaydar-'Alí if he might but read it. Mírzá Ḥaydar-'Alí agreed and, handing him the Tablet, pointed out that no Bahá'í document should fall into untrustworthy hands and that it was a necessary precaution that he not carry it on his person. He assured Fádil it would be delivered into his hands in due course.

With joy and excitement he read the Tablet, drinking in every word and allowing his spirit to bathe in the beauty and the blessings of its content. His heart was full as he discovered, with profound gratitude, that the answers to all of the questions he had been pondering were contained in the body of the Tablet.

Following is its text:

> The travelling Jináb-i-Fádil, upon him be the glory of God, the All-Glorious.
>
> He is God!
>
> O thou who hast beheld the mighty signs of thy Lord! It behoveth thee to raise the hands of gratitude to the heaven of Him Who is the All-Glorious, the Ever-Forgiving, and yield thanks that the veils have been rent asunder and the lights have shone forth, that the signs have been uncovered and the mysteries unravelled, and that thine eyes have been solaced

by the verses of thy Lord, the Help in Peril, the Unconstrained. Thus hath thine inner eye been illumined, thy heart found composure, thy soul gained confidence, and the fire of the love of God blazed in thy bosom.

Return then unto thy land, apprise the people of the advent of the days of God, and summon them unto His path through gentle admonitions and kindly utterances and through whatever is meet and seemly. Cast into the hearts a flame that will burn away the veils, disperse the mists, dispel the doubts, explain the allusions, proclaim the clear verses, expound the shining proofs, and pierce the darkness, that the light of truth may shine forth from all sides upon the embodiments of oneness.

'Abdu'l-Bahá, Abbás.

Twenty

The Rasht Incident

Fádil, as instructed by 'Abdu'l-Bahá, left 'Akká that same day for Rasht by way of Bádkubih and eventually arrived at the home of Mírzá Muhammad-'Alí Khán-i-Rashtí, a prominent Bahá'í of Rasht. Following consultation with the Local Spiritual Assembly he was asked to remain in that city to help with the teaching work. He did and as a result, not only was he able to excite and enthuse the believers there but to attract a great number of seekers. Many would come to hear him expound on the Bahá'í teachings and its claims using actual verses of the Qur'án as proof in his explanations. His fame grew and his reputation increased provoking the inevitable uproar among the city's clergy who, predictably, became inflamed with anger and jealousy.

Now there was at that time a very distinguished Bahá'í in Rasht by the name of Ibtiháju'l-Mulk, an historical figure in the Faith and very influential in Rasht. Seeing how the mullás had arisen against Fádil and were demonstrating great hostility towards him, he decided to send them a message stating that instead of causing such a tumult and commotion, they should come forward and discuss their objections and criticisms directly with Jináb-i-Fádil. At length, through the efforts of this noble and courageous Bahá'í several meetings were organized, one of them actually taking place inside the mosque. Each time Fádil, in the presence of the most skilled experts in religious jurisprudence, proved the truth and claims of the Bahá'í Cause. For their part the clergy, because of the wise and careful planning of these meetings by Ibtihaju'l-Mulk, were bound to respect and observe the conditions under which the arranged discussions took place. Eventually, defeated by virtue of Fádil's demonstrations, clear arguments and decisive proofs, his opponents were, one and all, reduced to silence.

Those confrontations increased Fádil's reputation and the story of his triumphs spread among the inhabitants of the city. Everywhere he went people would point him out to each other saying, "That's the man who exchanged arguments with our distinguished theologians and won."

But eventually bitterness and agitation among the populace waxed over the fact that a learned Bahá'í had repeatedly overcome the claims and arguments of their spiritual leaders. With disquiet mounting to the threshold of mob violence, the Local Spiritual Assembly of Rasht quickly decided that Fádil should leave for Tihrán and arranged for his clandestine departure.

After travelling some days on foot, Fádil arrived in Tihrán and soon contacted the Bahá'í Community. He became an active member, attending meetings and Nineteen day Feasts, giving classes and teaching courses. His presence brightened every meeting he attended and shed lustre on every gathering he was a part of. Indeed, his life amongst the friends there was the stimulus for a wonderful flourishing.

Twenty-One

Travel Teaching Assignments

Not many days after Fádil had settled into the Ṭihrán community the Local Spiritual Assembly of Ṭihrán received a Tablet from 'Abdu'l-Bahá. (Írán was not to form its first National Spiritual Assembly until 1933 at its first National Convention.) The Master's Tablet asked that a distinguished Bahá'í teacher be sent to proclaim the Faith in the city of Qum, a city renowned for its mosques and theological schools. When it was decided Jináb-i-Fádil was to go, he cheerfully accepted the mission and soon set out for Qum.

Arriving in the city he did not at first contact the Bahá'ís but rather took up residence in one of the Qum's theological schools. He volunteered to hold study classes and, from their outset, by drawing upon the wealth of his acquired learning, he was able to charm and enamour the most zealous and keen of the local theologians. As they shared their impressions and observations with one another they would say, "I swear I have seen no one who has researched and investigated the truth as he has."

It was, however, only a matter of time until Fádil's remarks and explanations were unable to hide the fact that it was his intention to teach the Bahá'í Faith. This provoked some amongst them who were mean and evil-minded to conspire against him and, in fact, initiate plans to kill him.

By this time he had established contact with the Local Spiritual Assembly of Qum, which, apprised of the situation, feared for his life and arranged for him to return to Ṭihrán. At the behest of the Spiritual Assembly he left Qum for the capital and, upon his arrival there, he was handed a Tablet which had been revealed by 'Abdu'l-Bahá in his honour and sent first to Rasht. It read:

> Rasht
> Care of Jináb-i-Ibtiháj
>
> The divine Jináb-i-Fádil of Shíráz, upon him be the glory of God, the All-Glorious!
>
> He is God!
>
> O divine scholar! Jináb-i-Ibtiháj hath written that even as a bright flame thou hast shone in the glass of Gílán, closed thine eyes to the ease and comfort of this fleeting world and to the praise of the inmates of this gloomy heap of dust, and that thou hast renounced and relinquished both heart and soul. All praise for this heartfelt endeavour of thine! "And amongst the people is he who forsaketh his self in his eagerness to behold the countenance of God."[11] Not until one acteth thus will the manifest light of God shine upon one's brow.

In an epistle addressed by the Ancient Beauty to a mystic, there appear the following lines:

Either adorn thyself as women do
Or choose man-like to take to the field

Praise God that thou hast spurred on thy charger in this field and, with the mallet of endeavour, carried away the ball of victory.

Abdu'l-Bahá, 'Abbás

In the days and weeks to come the Spiritual Assembly of Ṭihrán gave Fáḍil a series of travelling teaching assignments, among them were trips to the cities of Semnán and Sang-i-sar and in each of these, over a period of days, he fearlessly but with wisdom taught and proclaimed the Faith.

In most of the meetings his audiences were people from all walks of life and all shades of thought: agnostics, mystics and theologians. Special meetings, however, were set up for this learned servant of God to confront the most eminent and elite religious personalities of those respective cities, the illustrious "ullamá". In each of such meetings he would, with powerful and decisive language explain and expound the Bahá'í teachings, refute all misinterpretations of the Qur'án and win all arguments, silencing his opponents completely.

After Fáḍil returned to Ṭihrán another Tablet from the Master arrived for him. It was in answer to a letter of his own posing questions he had requested enlightenment on concerning a belief current among the Ithná-A<u>sh</u>aríyyih sect of Islám known as the "Sect of the Twelve", to do with the disappearance of the 12th Imám, the Qá'ím-i-Ál-i-Muḥammad (He Who arises out of the family of Muḥammad). The belief held by this sect is that the Imám disappeared into an under-ground passage in Surrá-man-Rá (Sámarrá) over a thousand years ago and still lives in one of those mysterious cities, Jábulqá and Jábulsá and will come forth in the fullness of time to fill the world with Justice.

In this letter Fádil, referring to the harbinger of the Báb's Revelation, "that luminous star of divine guidance, <u>Sh</u>ay<u>kh</u> Aḥmad-i-Aḥsá'í", asks 'Abdu'l-Bahá to "...graciously reveal the mysteries hidden in the allusions made by that light of knowledge and guidance regarding the twelfth Imám, the Qá'ím". Fádil, in his letter, goes on to say, "So far no one has unravelled the mysteries concealed within the allusions made by that source of knowledge and understanding. May 'Abdu'l-Bahá's pen which is the bearer of the Supreme Pen reveal the meaning of this mystery which would gladden the hearts of the friends and thereafter no one would put forth vain imaginings and worthless sayings." In the same letter Fádil had asked another question regarding the state, after death, of all those souls who remain heedless. What follows is the Master's reply:

Ṭihrán

His honour Fádil-i-Shírází, upon him be the glory of God!

He is God!

O thou who art attracted by the fragrances of God! I noted the contents of thine epistle and the purpose of thy call, and praised God for having inspired the pure in heart with divine susceptibilities and perfumed the senses of the people of light with a fragrance that hath enveloped the whole earth. I beseech Him to assist thee through that spirit which quickeneth the hearts, the minds, and the souls of men. He, verily, is wont to hear and to answer the prayers of whomsoever invoketh Him.

Thou hadst asked concerning the twelfth Imám. Know thou that this perception did not originally exist in the physical world. The twelfth Imám existed in the Unseen realm, but had no reality on the material plane. However, some of the Shí'ah elders of the time deemed it advisable, solely for the protection of the weak elements among the people, to portray a person existing in the Unseen realm as being possessed of a corporal existence. "For the world of existence is a single world; it cannot be hidden, except from your eyes, and cannot be manifest, except to your eyes." Such was their thought, their perception, and their design. Ibn-i-Hajar hath a verse in the Sawá'iq, saying:

A cellar cannot engender a creature such
As fancy prompteth you to call a man, O fools!
May then your feeble minds be excused, for ye have
Added a third to the phoenix and the ghouls.

In any case, were one to refer to the accounts and carefully reflect upon their meaning, it would become clear and evident that this magnanimous Imám, peace be upon him, hath never existed in the physical realm.

As to the question of the immortality of negligent souls once they have cast off their earthly frame, their immortality is tantamount to extinction, inasmuch as they are deprived of a heavenly life. They are even as the mineral, which endureth in the mineral realm, but which is utter nonexistence when compared to human existence. The other worlds are not a place where realities are transformed, or natures transmuted, or creation renewed. It is clear, however, that souls will progress in degrees and become the object of divine pardon and forgiveness.

This reply hath been made brief due to lack of time. Through careful thought and examination thou wilt no doubt elucidate and elaborate upon it.

For now, choose Ṭihrán as thy place of residence. From time to time, do thou travel to one of the other provinces and return. Convey

My loving greetings to Fathu'lláh Khán-i-Mushír. His presence here would not be advisable at this time. God willing, in due course permission will be granted.

Abdu'l-Bahá, Abbás

Twenty-Two

Matrimony

The instructions at the end of the above Tablet made it clear to Fádil he was to make Ṭihrán his place of residence and the centre of his teaching activities, with occasional teaching trips to other centres.

In the light of these recent directives, a vision of his future began to unfold. The more he thought about it the more he found himself thinking that it would be good to find a wife and establish himself. Some of his close friends from among the believers, those with whom he shared the content of the recent Tablet, on becoming aware of the Master's instructions to Fádil, encouraged him to settle down and in fact were actively in search of the 'right' match for him. But they realized that getting him married was no small task considering Fádil's lack of any material means, his ever increasing travelling teaching assignments and his all-consuming interest and yearning to reach higher stages of spiritual consciousness. It would be necessary to find, in the partner they were looking for, intelligence, education, spiritual-mindedness, complete devotion to the Faith and a detachment from material ease and comfort equal to his. It was not until after some considerable searching that they all came to the same conclusion: his marriage partner would have to be the young niece of the illustrious Fá'izih Khánum, a highly devoted and audacious Bahá'í teacher.

Fádil wished 'Abdu'l-Bahá to know that he was content with the will of God in marrying and would continue, supported by his partner, his work of travelling and teaching the Cause. In the following letter which Fádil wrote to the Master he reveals his transparent honesty and acquiescence in God as he explains how it was that the particular young woman to whom he had become engaged was found and how she had accepted his proposal in complete trust that God would provide for them despite Fádil's lack of means.

> He is God!
>
> O my Master, my Refuge, my Asylum and my Shelter. Praise be to God, a praise that is seemly and in His good pleasure, that on Saturday, the second of Shav'val 1326 (Sept. 25th 1908), in accordance with His desire and will and without any will of this evanescent servant, by approval of a group of trustees and Hands of the Cause of God and upon the good will of the respected leaf Fá'izih Khánum and Jináb-i-Áqá Siyyid Ṣádiq (her husband) and by the encouragement and approval of Jináb-i-Mírzá Ḥassan Khán (Adíb, Hand of the Cause) and his brother Jináb-i-Áqá Mírzá Abdu'l-Bághí Khán and with the assistance and total support of Jináb-i-Mirzá Javád, the niece of Fá'izih Khánum, who's name is Naw-Zuhúr Bagum, was betrothed to this poor one. But at the

beginning of the consultations some considered this action contrary to wisdom due to the lack of means of this servant, while others, setting their sight upon the All-Provider viewed it right.

Jináb-i-Mírzá Ḥassan Khán said that the matter should be put to Naw-Zuhúr Bagum to see if she would be content in spite of his poverty. They went to discuss the matter with her returning with the news that she was aware of my poverty and wanted nothing from me and that she accepted the proposal for the sake of God and that God was potent to provide the daily necessities. So, this servant also placing his trust in God, accepted the matter. It gave me assurance that because Fá'izih Khánum is herself a teacher of the Cause and her niece is educated, that she would support me in arising to teach the Cause. I made the condition that whenever I wanted to travel for the purpose of teaching the Cause she would not object. I hope this meets with Thy good pleasure.

" O my God, O my God, look not upon my hopes and my doings, nay rather look upon Thy will that hath encompassed the heavens and the earth. By Thy most Great Name O Thou Lord of all Nations, I have desired only what Thou didst desire and love only what Thou dost love."

Thy poor servant,
Fádil-i-Shírází

As Fádil had mentioned in his letter to the Master the young Naw-Zuhúr was well aware of his lack of material means. While she had heard of Fádil's vast knowledge and the eloquence with which he expounded the Bahá'í teachings before the Muslim clerics and divines, refuting all their arguments, it is likely her own spiritual upbringing had reminded her of Baha'u'lláh's counsel, "Put thy whole confidence in the grace of God, thy Lord. Let Him be thy trust in whatever thou doest, and be of them that have submitted themselves to His Will....for with Him are the treasuries of the heavens and the earth. He bestoweth them upon whom He will..."[12] and "Great is the blessedness awaiting the poor that endure patiently and conceal their sufferings...."[13] Quite possibly, upon hearing through her aunt and uncle of Fádil's request for her hand in marriage, she would have remembered a dream in which her deceased father told her that he was coming to be with her and protect her (more will be said about this in the next chapter).

There is no account of events relating to the period after their engagement or of the marriage ceremony itself. One can but imagine it to have been simple, honoured by the presence of the Hands of the Cause of God and all those distinguished individuals who, as Fádil's letter indicates, had advised the two of them and approved of their union. One might expect also that the same beloved friends would have chanted the beautiful marriage prayers and thereby have added to the ceremony's befitting atmosphere of spirituality.

After the couple had been married and were living in Ṭihrán, Fádil was approached by the Local Spiritual

93

Assembly of Ṭihrán to consider teaching at the Tarbíyat Bahá'í School, for boys. Fáḍil accepted the offer and was employed there to teach Arabic and Persian literature.

It should be explained that this was the first school owned and operated by the Bahá'í Community of Írán. In the words of Shoghi Effendi, "It was during this period, at a time when state schools and colleges were practically non-existent in that country (Írán) and when the education given in existing religious institutions was lamentably defective, that its (the Faith's) earliest schools were established, beginning with the Tarbíyat schools in Ṭihrán, one for boys and one for girls, followed by the Ta'yíd and Mawhibat schools in Hamadán, the Vahdat-i-Bashar school in Káshán and other similar educational institutions in Bárfurúsh and Qazvin."[14]

At that time the Tarbíyat school for girls had not yet been established in Ṭihrán and it was a few years later, in 1911, that through the special support and encouragement of 'Abdu'l-Bahá the school opened and Fáḍil began teaching classes there as well. It was in that same year that the couple was blessed with a child, a girl they called Subhaníyyih, (she who is praised).

To assist in understanding the nature of the couple's relationship with each other, their children and the Bahá'í community, the next chapter will be devoted to a brief account of Naw-Zuhúr's life of service to her beloved Faith and family.

Twenty-Three
Her Dream Shaped Her Life

Naw-Zuhúr, meaning New Dawn, was born in the year 1892 to a distinguished Persian family. Her maternal grandfather, Áqá Mírzá Muḥammad-Ḥusayn, was a descendent of the Imáms and a renowned theologian of Iṣfahán. There will be more of him said in the last section in this book.

During Naw-Zuhúr's childhood years cholera, without a cure, had been occurring sporadically throughout Írán just as it had been for decades. It was after the ascension of Bahá'u'lláh that one such epidemic struck most provinces killing a great number of people. It seemed that every household was hit by the deadly disease and lost one or more of its members. Each family was in mourning, everyone wore black, mosques and other buildings in the stricken cities were shrouded in black cloth and people everywhere were beseeching and imploring the Almighty for help. The situation grew increasingly worse with encroaching summer heat.

It was during a similar period, when cholera was rampant, that Naw-Zuhúr lost both of her parents, each succumbing to the deadly disease within a week of each other. It is not clear what age she was when she and her sister were orphaned; it was, nevertheless, to the home of their maternal aunt, Fá'izih <u>Kh</u>ánum, that they were then taken; an aunt who was willing to commit herself to the raising of the two girls. (A vignette of the eventful and heroic life of Fá'izih <u>Kh</u>ánum is to be found in the Appendix).

Thus it was that Naw-Zuhúr, under the guidance of her aunt, not only a learned and devoted maidservant of the Cause but a renowned Bahá'í teacher, was raised in a distinctly Bahá'í environment and in due course became well educated, this at a time when women in Írán received little if any formal education and that which they did receive invariably never went beyond primary school.

It was Naw-Zuhúr's aunt and uncle who, when Naw-Zuhúr was sixteen years of age, came to her with the news of a request from Jináb-i-Fádil for her hand in marriage. As a younger teenager Naw-Zuhúr had dreamt of a man she believed to be her father, and who, in the dream, uttered these comforting words, "Do not worry my child; you need not grieve, for I am coming to be with you". It was not long after that dream that the young woman saw Jináb-i-Fádil for the first time and realized, to her astonishment, that his features were the same as those of the man in her dream. She was to be further amazed when she would learn that the given names of her father and Fádil-i-<u>Sh</u>írází, the one of whose reputation and fame as a leading Bahá'í teacher she had been well aware, were the same—Ibráhím.

She realized then the meaning of her dream and the comforting promise of her father, for Fádil, as her father would have been, was some years her senior. That Fádil was poor, as she was informed by her devoted aunt and uncle, was of little consequence in making her decision. The conviction in her own heart was confirmed by the encouraging words of the loved ones who conveyed to her the marriage proposal. She accepted it, saying to her aunt and uncle, "I accept this to be the will of God; I know he is poor but I do not expect anything. I trust the Lord and he will provide."

Some time after the above-mentioned dream she sent a supplication to 'Abdu'l-Bahá through Fá'izih Khánum, who was often in correspondence with the Master, asking forgiveness and pardon for her father. She received the following prayer in reply:

Ṭihrán

Care of the handmaiden of God, Fá'izih

The handmaiden of God, Naw-Zuhúr, upon her be the glory of God.

He is God!

O God, My God!

This Thy handmaiden hath believed in Thy beauty and hath acknowledged Thy signs. She hath sought the Threshold of Thy mercy and turned towards the Kingdom of Thy lordship. She hath interceded on behalf of her father, relying upon Thy forgiveness and pardon and supplicating Thy favour and bounty. O Lord! I cover my face in the dust of submission to Thy celestial Glory, beseeching Thee to forgive and pardon her father and to shelter him beneath the canopy of Thine abounding grace within Thy garden of repose. Supply him, O God, with every gift and blessing in Thine all-highest Paradise.

Thou, verily, art the Generous, the Compassionate, the Pardoner, the Ever-Forgiving, the One Whose help is implored by all.

'Abdu'l-Bahá, Abbás

From the beginning of her union with Jináb-i-Fádil, Naw-Zuhúr did her utmost to serve him while at the same time remain in the service of her beloved Faith.

Learning Arabic under his tutelage (It should be understood that Arabic is a Semitic language, a very difficult one and very different from the Persian language which is Indo-European) was an accomplishment which proved to be of great assistance to Naw-Zuhúr, not only in better understanding the Kitáb-i-Aqdas, the Most Holy Book, but all other Revelation writings in Arabic, including the Qur'án, the Muslim Holy Book. Her knowledge of Arabic allowed her, some years later, to use its texts to prove the Faith of Bahá'u'lláh in the firesides and deepenings she gave. It was especially useful to her in conducting study classes on the Most Holy Book, the Kitáb-i-Aqdas, for at that time it existed only in Arabic.

During the early years of their life together Fádil was employed as a teacher at the Tarbiyat Bahá'í School where he taught courses in Arabic and in

Persian Literature. Because he devoted his evenings to conducting Bahá'í meetings he was very much in demand as a speaker at firesides in Bahá'í homes, at deepenings, special gatherings and at study classes for adults and youth alike when large numbers would assemble to hear him speak.

By the time the couple's daughter and firstborn, Subháníyyih, was eight years old and their son, 'Abdu'lláh, was three, the Spiritual Assembly of Ṭihrán consulted with them on relocating and establishing themselves in the city of Hamadán.*

In response to the Assembly's request they moved to Hamadán and soon thereafter Fádil was teaching at the Ta'yíd Bahá'í School for Boys. Fortuitously, Naw-Zuhúr found employment at another school in Hamadán, the Mawhibat Bahá'í School for Girls, where there was an opportunity for her to take up duties as its principal.

Life for them in Hamadán was not easy; in addition to the demands of their jobs and of raising two children, much of their free time was spent teaching the Faith and struggling to strengthen the Bahá'í Community there, many of whose members were of Jewish background (the city had a sizeable Jewish minority who had lived there since the Fifth Century A.D.)

*This city in mid-western Írán is situated on a high plain and is dominated by the 3580m. Mount Alvand. Hamadán's weather is cold from September to May and there is plenty of snow. Its interesting history goes back to at least the second century B.C. when it was founded by King Jamshid. It was the median capital under Cyrus the Great in the Sixth Century B.C. when the city was known as Ecbátáná (meeting place).

Fádil had written 'Abdu'l-Bahá and explained some
of the difficulties and hardships that he and the family
were going through in Hamadán. No doubt the following Tablet from the Master brought great joy, composure and solace to the couple as their souls were
nourished by His words:

> Jináb-i-Fádil and his honoured spouse, upon
> them be the glory of God, the All-Glorious!
>
> He is God!
>
> O My Lord and My Desire! These, verily,
> are two birds whose hearts have longed for the
> bowers of Thy oneness, whose souls have been
> attracted to the meadows of Thy mercy, and
> who are ablaze with the fire of Thy love amidst
> Thy creatures.
>
> O Lord! Assist them at all times and under
> all conditions. Revive their hearts through the
> soft breezes of the morn and the sweet savours
> of fragrant flowers. Thou, verily, art their
> solace at such times when their plight waxeth
> more grievous day and night. Bestow Thy grace
> upon them, O Lord, and unlock before them
> the doors of Thy providence through Thy
> favour and bounty. Grant their desires
> through Thine unfailing grace and relieve their
> plight through Thy surpassing munificence.
>
> O Lord! Turn their adversities into ease and
> comfort and their trials and tribulations into
> peace and prosperity. Prepare for them the
> path and pave for them the way.

Thou, verily, art the Beneficent, the All-Bounteous, the Almighty, the Most Generous. No God is there save Thee, the Most Compassionate, the All-Merciful.

As to the allocation for the survivors of Sadru's-Sudúr, a separate letter will be written. Upon you rest the glory of glories.

'Abdu'l-Bahá, Abbás

Fádil, as always, regularly reported to 'Abdu'l-Bahá any important incidents in connection with the Bahá'í schools or the Bahá'í Community, asking His advice and beseeching His guidance and blessings. In the following Tablet 'Abdu'l-Bahá responds to such reports with exhortations and advice, bright beacons of guidance by which the couple tried diligently to live and to apply in all aspects of their lives.

Jináb-i-Fádil-i-Shírází, upon him be the glory of God!

He is God!

O My Lord and My Desire!

Thou knowest well My love for Thy loved ones, and My care for Thy cherished ones, and Mine ardent supplication that Thou wouldst make them to be the signs of Thy mercy amongst Thy people and the ensigns of Thy knowledge amidst Thy creatures.

Among Thy loved ones is this servant of Thine, humble before Thy word, lowly at Thy threshold, who proclaimeth Thy proofs and who spreadeth abroad Thy fragrances. O God, My God! Assure his heart, comfort his soul, console his spirit, and bestow Thy blessings upon his daily affairs. Grant him to rejoice in Thine abundant grace; give him to delight in Thy favours amongst Thy creatures both in the visible and the invisible realm; and assist him to exert a worthy endeavour in Thy service.

Thou, verily, art the All-Glorious, the Ever-Forgiving.

O Jináb-i-Fádil! It behoveth us to turn our eyes towards the Scene of supernal glory, that we may behold the lights of divine assistance shining above the unseen Horizon. Whatsoever Thou desirest, ask it of God; whatsoever thou seekest, seek it from Him. Be confident and composed; be submissive and steadfast. With all thy heart and soul be thou a sincere friend and a loving companion unto all, and show forth such deeds as are worthy of the divine Threshold. If thou perceivest from any soul the fragrances of God, unloose thy tongue in his glorification and praise, but otherwise remain silent. Nay, should a soul find fault with thee, praise him instead; should he condemn thee, commend him in return; should he commit an iniquity, show forth justice in exchange. For such are the characteristics of the favoured ones of God and such is the hallmark of them that are devoted unto Him. Blessed is he who evinceth such attributes amongst the people.

Upon thee be salutations and praise!

'Abdu'l-Bahá, 'Abbás

The extreme difficulties they faced those three years they were in Hamadán, due to reasons both in and outside the Bahá'í community, were extremely stressful ones. This and the meagre salary the school could afford to pay, which barely allowed them to make ends meet, eventually prompted their decision to return to Țihrán. This would be a journey which was to hold for them many treacherous difficulties each of which would be overcome with fortitude, resignation and patience until at length, weary but with hope and anticipation they would reach the capital.

***

Naw-Zuhúr's experience of teaching and supervising at the Mawhibat School for Girls in Hamadán proved useful back in Țihrán where she was able to draw upon it in conducting Bahá'í classes for the education of children, especially young girls, and in her teaching at the Tarbiyat school for girls. She had a gift for storytelling and a special gift for communicating with children who delighted in sitting at her feet listening to her stories.

In November of 1924, over two years after their return from Hamadán, Naw-Zuhúr gave birth to a baby girl whom they named Rúháníyyih.

103

The writer's memory of her grandmother is of one from whom great composure and inner happiness radiated, of one whose life was characterized by simplicity and who was content with very little, who had surrendered her will to the will of God, had truly detached herself from the world and was entirely occupied in the service of her Lord.

Naw-Zuhúr's selfless devotion and love may be highlighted by a particular example wherein she undertook to look after two young daughters of a great and revered teacher of the Faith whose name was Jináb-i-Sadru's-Sudúr. One can only imagine what a flood of joy, confirmation and encouragement she felt when she received a Tablet from 'Abdu'l-Bahá showering her with bounty and praise for the care she had given the two children. The translated Tablet reads:

Ṭihrán

Care of Ḥájí Mirzá 'Abdu'lláh

The honoured and respected spouse of Jináb-i-Fádil-i-Shírází, upon her be the glory of God, the All-Glorious!

He is God!

O favoured handmaiden of God! Jináb-i-Fádil hath written concerning the services thou hast rendered to the daughters of his honour Sadru's-Sudúr. The hearts were moved at the news that, praise be to God, the favoured maidservants of the Lord of glory have been enabled to render the most distinguished services, to perform the most noble deeds, and, in particular, to educate the daughters of one who was the greatest among the signs of God and the most illustrious of His ensigns. Such care and attention shall indeed be the cause of nearness to the incomparable Lord. Wherefore be happy and rejoice, and be free of all sorrow and grief, for engaging in such service and for partaking of such unfailing bounty. Those young ones are indeed the children and kindred of this sorely tested Servant, and I am most pleased and grateful for thy services. Render thanks unto God for being the recipient of such words. Upon thee be the glory of glories.

'Abdu'l-Bahá, Abbás

It was on the twenty eighth of November 1921, while the Fádil family was still in Hamadán, that the Bahá'í world was stunned by the news of the passing of His Holiness, 'Abdu'l-Bahá. The news came as a thunderbolt and shook every heart to its depths. His departure from this ephemeral world to the world divine occurred so suddenly and so unexpectedly that the whole Bahá'í community was shattered with grief, hearts were sore distressed and eyes overflowed with bitter tears. Yet in spite of it all, love, unity and a great desire for service to His Cause was apparent among the Bahá'ís and when news of the appointment by 'Abdu'l-Bahá, in His Will and Testament, of His grandson Shoghi Effendi Rabbání as the Guardian reached the believers in Írán they rallied behind him and, unified, they arose to serve under his guidance with faithfulness, devotion and renewed vigour, re-dedicating themselves to the service of the Cause.

The Fádil family, though overwhelmed by grief and sadness upon hearing the news, were resigned to the Will of God, loyal to His blessed Cause and were confirmed in the Covenant. Their depth of love and devotion toward the young Guardian Shoghi Effendi is apparent in the following supplication addressed to him a few years later by Naw-Zuhúr Khánum.

O my Master!

O thou Master of the Righteous! O thou who knowest the secrets!

Although the pleadings of these servants cause trouble and inconvenience to that Holy Being of the Divine Beneficence, what recourse have I? Unto whom can I turn but Thee?

"'Tis no wonder if thy lovers round thy
threshold crowd,
Flies gather wherever sweets are found."

These weak ones, severed from all people and all things are holding unto the hem of thy robe the most pure. Night and day they regard as sweet nectar the affliction of sorrows and the bitterness of separation; under all conditions they trust His hidden mercies.

The spouse of this lowly one, Fádil-i-Shírází, although spending every minute of his life in service to the Holy Threshold, regards himself unworthy of mention at thy radiant presence

through offering his humble supplication
which is the duty of every servant, every afflicted and distraught one. Therefore as this handmaiden, despaired at gaining, through him,
acceptance among thy handmaidens and to be
counted among thy ancient servants, has put
forth the step of courage and dared to write,
with a broken pen, these few words from the
recesses of her weary heart.

Perchance through the glances of that
knower of secrets and Guardian of the Cause
of the One True God, this unknown handmaiden, her kind spouse and their three off-
springs, Subháníyyih, 'Abdu'lláh and
Rúháníyyih, may attain the utmost desire of
them that are nigh unto Him, that absolute
nothingness, the pure and absolute certitude,
those means of attaining to the good pleasure
of the Best Beloved. He granteth His Mercy
unto whomsoever He willeth. He is the
Knower, apprised of all.

The handmaid of Thy threshold,
Naw-Zuhúr

Subháníyyih graduated from the Tarbiyat School in
1930-31 and, as her beautiful handwriting revealed
her great talent in the art of calligraphy the school,
almost immediately, approached her to teach calligraphy classes.

A word about this impressive art; calligraphy,
especially in the "Nasta'liq" style, had been developed
and practiced among the Persians from as far back as

107

the thirteenth century. Educated members within good families were expected to have very good hand-writing and the foundation of this particular form of handwriting, Nasta'liq, was laid through the exercises and training that the students received at school. In the advanced classes the students were trained in its broken form called, "Shikastih", which is a much faster and free style of writing.

The pen, ink and paper used by Persian calligraphers were made of particular materials; the pen was fashioned from a thin brown reed cut and stubbed with a sharp knife. The ink used was made from a special black powder to which water was added, and the mixture poured into a small glass bottle. When not in use it was kept beside a lacquered pen box that housed pen reeds of different sizes. Nowadays ready-mixed fluid ink is used while commercially made papers replace the hand made variety previously used.

In October of 1933 a joyous event took place in Fádil's family which was the marriage of Subháníyyih to a young man by the name of 'Alí Faláhí who had in fact embraced the Faith through Fádil himself and had become a very devoted Bahá'í, although his entire family remained devout Muslims.

Subháníyyih had been the youngest teacher at the school during her two years of teaching and was very much loved by the students. Once married she had to quit her job and accompany her husband because of a job related transfer to the southern city of Ahváz. Fortunately with the couple returning to Ṭihrán the following year, the separation from her beloved family was not long lasting. Sadly however it was in December of that year, 1934, that by order of the governmental authorities, all nineteen Bahá'í schools in Írán were shut down; Bahá'í schools closing for Bahá'í Holy days was the pretext given. Subháníyyih's experience in teaching at that early age helped her to become involved in Bahá'í education in general and with children in particular, some years later.

Naw-Zuhúr was only 43 in 1935 when her beloved Fáḍil passed away. After his passing she devoted herself even more to teaching the Faith. Conducting regular firesides on an ongoing basis in a number of Bahá'í homes spread across the City of Ṭihrán, she would make her way to them on foot or by public transportation regardless of weather conditions and despite, at times, her fragile health. So able was she in these meetings, at giving clear and convincing proofs of the truth of the Bahá'í Revelation and explaining how it fulfilled the prophesies in the Qur'án and other Islámic traditions regarding the coming of the Promised One, that through her firesides many seekers over the years have embraced the Faith.

Besides her great ability as a fireside speaker Naw-Zuhúr had a talent for matchmaking. A young man knew that if she were to present his request in asking the parents of the young woman of his choice for their daughter's hand in marriage, consent would most surely be forthcoming. Of course she would only act in such cases as she thought the young man to be deserving. Always, if she succeeded in helping the match to materialize, she would be one of the honoured guests at the marriage ceremony.

Often accompanying her places were her two grand-daughters, Houri and Pari and it always delighted them the many times they were taken along to the marriages she attended. Although wedding festivities in Írán tended, in general, to be rather elaborate affairs, the young girls looked forward to them with great excitement not only because of the fun, the entertainment and the vast array of delectable goodies they would find at them but also because of their grandmother's young and happy spirit.

At age fifty-seven a sudden heart attack brought Naw-Zuhúr's earthly life to an end and she passed away peacefully in the arms of her oldest daughter, Subháníyyih, with her grand daughter Houri standing by the bedside.

A huge crowd of friends and strangers, admirers and acquaintances, young and old, high and low, attended the funeral. There were so many people that large busses had to be hired to transport most of the crowd to the Bahá'í cemetery, Gulistán-i-Jávíd (The Eternal Flower Garden) outside Ṭihrán. With the great hall completely filled and many standing, they listened as Jináb-i-'Alí-Akbar Furutan, Secretary of the National Spiritual Assembly and later elevated to Hand of the Cause, paid tribute to Naw-Zuhúr Khánum. He extolled her radiant spirit, her selfless devotion and unquestioned loyalty to the Master and the beloved Guardian; he celebrated her tireless zeal and her unfailing sacrificial efforts in teaching and propagating the Faith, which resulted in the enrolment of great numbers. He recalled how she continued to travel to all parts of the city on crowded busses or on foot, despite ill health or severe weather conditions, to host her weekly firesides. The words of Jináb-i-Furutan still echo in the mind of the writer, who was, at the time, about thirteen years of age.

The earthly life of Naw-Zuhúr thus honoured, her remains were interred in the Bahá'í Cemetary alongside those of Jináb-i-Fádil. Her saintly spirit had winged its flight from its mortal cage to continue its eternal union with that of her beloved husband and in the company of all the great souls gone before her.

Memorial meetings continued over the next several days in order to accommodate the many who wished to pay homage to her treasured memory.

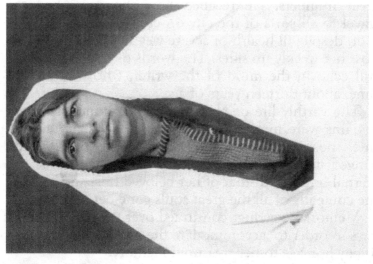

Naw-Zuhúr Khánum sometime after her marriage to Fáḍil

Fáḍil-i-Shírází in the 1920s

Naw-Zuhúr with a group of believers in 1937-38 seated 4th from left, behind her (seated) is Abú'l-Qásim Faizí, later appointed Hand of the Cause of God. Standing (to his right) Gloria, his wife and (to his left) Rúhániyih Fádil

Abdu'lláh Fádil in 1941   Rúháníyyih Fádil-Fáregh

Subháníyyih Fádil-Faláhí
on a visit to Shíráz in 1938

114

Naw-Zuhúr (center) with her daughters Subhániyyih (on her right)
and Rúhániyyih (on her left), standing front are granddaughters
Houri (left) and Pari

Naw-Zuhúr with grand-
daughter Pari

Olfatíyyih Mihrabán,
Naw-Zuhúr's sister

Naw-Zuhúr Khánum about 1945-46

Group of teachers with the 8th grade students at
Tarbiyat School about 1919,(from left to right) Sultan-Khattátin, Fuád Ashraf, 'Abbás Forát, Fádili-
Shírázi,Nasru'lláh Mavedat, 'Abdu'lláh Ráhemi, Mirzá Mihdí Rahbar (vice Principal) top row (center)
Abú'l-Qásim Faizí

117

Some of the staff of Tarbiyat school, early 1930s (Front row right to left)
Siyyid 'Abbás Alaví, Ziyáu'lláh Nabil-i-Akbar, Fádil-i-Shírází, Azízu'lláh
Messbáh (principal), Sultán-Khattátin, Hidáyatu'lláh Qá'im-Maqámí, next,
unidentified. (back row 1st from right) Dr. Massíh Farhangí martyred during
the Islamic Revolution in Írán, 5th 'Alí-Muḥammad Varqá

Delegates at the 1st National Convention of Írán, April 1933,
Fádil is seated in the front row (2nd from left)

118

Members of the Board of Ṭihrán Teaching Council 1931-32 Fáḍil seated second row (far right) and seated next to him is Azizu'lláh Messbáh

119

Fádil-i-Shírází in 1934, one year before his death

National Teaching Committee of Írán, 1934-35
Fádil seated 3rd from left

National Bahá'í Education Committee of Írán, 1940 (Seated from right) Attáu'lláh Muqarrabí,(unidentified), Subháníyyih Fádil-Faláhí Rúhangíz Fatheazam, (?), Emái, (back row 2nd from right) Músá Amánat, Hádi Rahmání, 4th&5th unidentified, 6th Muqbil, (?)

National Bahá'í Education Committee of Írán, 1946-47
(Seated from right) Áfághíyyih Naímí, Subháníyyih Fádil-Faláhí,
Colonel Sohráb, Attáu'lláh Muqarrabí, Báhirih Arjomand,
Emáí, (standing from right), Massrour, 'Abbás-Qulí Rúhání,
Talí'ih Mavaddat, Ihsrághián?, Táhirih Aláí, Músá Amánat Behín-áin

The Bahá'í Children Education Committee of Ṭihrán 1945-46
Subháníyyih Fádil-Faláhí (back row 2nd from left)

122

A family photo taken in early 1950s, Subháníyyih (seated center) with her husband 'Alí Faláhí, daughters Houri to his right and Pari to his left, (standing front) their son Farámarz and daughter Minou

Twenty-Four

The Two Cousins

Besides teaching at the Tarbíyat School for boys
and girls Fádil had engaged in giving firesides during
the evenings in various established Bahá'í homes
throughout the city. Often among those attending the
meetings were learned theologians and distinguished
personalities and, as one might imagine, the conversa-
tional exchanges were riveting for all present.

At one fireside gathering where Fádil was speaking
there were two mullás (Muslim theologians) who happened to be cousins. The one who seemed the older
and wiser of the two confronted Fádil with the question, "What reason can you give us to explain why you
came to believe in this Cause?"

"Proofs and evidences of this Most Great Cause
are many", answered Fádil, "but the foremost and
greatest among them is the torrent of Revelation
which has poured from the Pen and the Tongue of the
Manifestation Himself, whose knowledge was not
acquired but innate."

"Can you give us an example of what he revealed?"
queried the mullá.

124

Fádil replied, "Here are some of the revealed words of His Holiness, Bahá'u'lláh", and then proceeded, reverently and with deep and sincere conviction, to chant The Tablet of Aḥmad, which he had committed to memory.

The mullá's response was to bluster, "If this be revelation then I too can utter the like of it".

"If you immediately with neither hesitation nor reflection", returned Fádil, "utter words of your own such as these, I promise that I, upon the instant, will believe in you."

"Very well", was the mullá's reply; he then arose, gathered his cloak and knelt down. After a second or two he cleared his throat, caressed his beard and began with a Salavát, a special formulistic praise and greeting to God, Muḥammad and His Descendants; the actual words he used are the opening words of the Qur'án. He waited. After a minute or so had passed he placed both hands on the floor and removed himself from the place he had been kneeling to another spot a meter away where he again knelt erectly, stroked his moustache and beard, repeated the Salavát then waited; nothing. He moved again, repeated the ritual, nothing. His mind was blank; no words came to him. Again he moved and again repeated the Salavát. Again there was nothing.

Fádil observed the scene quietly. As the mullá shifted for the fourth time and while the Salavát was still on his lips the other mullá burst into laughter, chortling, "Cousin, if you can't reveal anything you can at least cease your Salavát repetition!"

Twenty-Five

A Dream Shared

Fádil's experiences of visions and dreams continued throughout his life; some of them he shared with
his family and were written down as keepsakes. One
for example, was a dream in which he saw a young
man around whose collar he noticed embroidered
verses sewn on with green thread. In the dream he
thought the young man to be the Qá'ím. The youth
was positioned in a way that would allow Fádil to read
the verses and before the dream ended he had been
able to read one completely. It was poetry. He inscribed the words upon waking and later that day
shared the verse with his friend, Jináb-i-'Azíz'u'lláh
Messbáh, a distinguished Bahá'í and Principal of the
Tarbiyat School. The Principal added his own verse
marrying it well with the first and to that Fádil added
two of his own. He then wrote 'Abd'u'l-Bahá concerning the matter and included the verses.

Here is a rough translation of Fádil's poem:

O Thou Revealer and Manifest Sustainer,
Glory and Sublimity are Thine.

By Thy light the sources of light and
wisdom are illumined.
O my Master, all titles circumambulate
around Thee,
And Thou hast chosen the title of the
Servant of Bahá.
All being doth witness Thy Sovereignty,
Who hast granted guidance and
steadfastness to them that are nigh unto Thee.

And here is 'Abdu'l-Bahá's reply to Fádil:

Ṭihrán

Jináb-i-Fádil-i-Shírází

He is God!

A letter was written to thee a few days ago
and dispatched through Jináb-i-Amín. Now,
thy most recent letter hath been perused. The
poems thou didst compose in the realm of
dreams have been recorded in the Book of the
Unseen and shall not vanish from memory.

God be praised, thou art engaged in serving
at the Tarbíyat School and occupied with the
service of the Cause. Thou art instructing the
young women and expounding the luminous
verses of God unto them. To the handmaidens
of God, Rúhangíz Khánum, Zahrá Khánum,
Maryam Khánum, Ishráqíyyih Khánum,
Shawkat Khánum, Batúl Khánum, Farahangíz
Khánum, Rúháníyyih Khánum, Subháníyyih
Khánum, Naw-Zuhúr Khánum, do Thou
convey My fondest greetings.

127

My hope is that day by day they shall grow more assiduous in their studies and benefit from thine utterances and elucidations. Upon thee be the glory of glories.

'Abdu'l-Bahá, Abbás.

Many years had passed since Fádil had received any news of his family. The one person in particular, whose health and welfare was of much concern to him, was his mother. It was, eventually, through the visit of some relatives who came to Ṭihrán and were able to establish contact with him, that he became aware of his mother's condition and how much their separation had affected her especially since, according to her husband's wishes, she had not been allowed to even mention her son's name or talk about him within the household after he had joined the Bahá'í Faith. Upon learning of this Fádil wrote to the Master requesting Him to reveal a prayer by means of which he could beseech pardon and forgiveness for his mother. What follows is the response from 'Abdu'l-Bahá:

Ṭihrán

To the attention of Jináb-i-Fádil-i-Shírází, upon him be the glory of God, the All-Glorious.

Prayer of forgiveness for the mother of Jináb-i-Fádil, upon her be the glory of God, the All-Glorious.

He is God!

O God, My God!

This is one of Thy humble and lowly maid-servants who hath fervently prayed to the kingdom of Thy unity. She hath implored Thee in the heart of dawn, and besought Thee in the dark of night and at the height of day, relying upon Thee and imploring Thy forgiveness and pardon.

O Lord! The ocean of Thy pardon hath surged before Thy servants and the breezes of Thy forgiveness have wafted over Thy cherished handmaidens. O Lord, deprive not this poor one of Thy boundless favours. Abandon her not, lifeless and weak, abased and fallen, to the abyss of shame and degradation, but shelter her through Thy mercy in the garden of Thy forgiveness and pardon, and destine for her all that is good and seemly in the paradise of Thy good-pleasure. Thou, verily, art the All-Bountiful, the All-Glorious, the Most Merciful.

Abdu'l-Bahá, Abbás

His mother passed away a few years later but his father lived a long life and died at the age of one hundred and ten.

Twenty-Six

Confrontation

Among some incidents of interest in the life of Fádil around that period is the story of his confrontation with two Muslim clergy of Sangalaj. First, however, it will be helpful to understand the circumstances which caused that meeting to take place.

Sangalaj was a district of Ṭihrán, where the poor and illiterate population was receptive to the corrupting influences of religious leaders whose practice it was to attack the Bahá'í Faith from the pulpits of the mosques with slander and false accusations. Among such of the district's clergy around the year 1337 A.H. (about 1918) were two vile and ignoble brothers by the names of Ḥájí Áqá Riḍá and Shaykh Muḥammad. The malignant intent of these two was to provoke and challenge the Bahá'í representatives to come forward to argue and, in the ensuing battle of words, to inflict upon them defeat and public humiliation. Because of the extreme danger, which did not rule out physical violence, the Bahá'ís did not deem confrontation with the two mullás advisable.

Finally one day the distinguished and learned Jináb-i-Mírzá Ḥassan-i-Adib, a Hand of the Cause, volunteer-

130

ed to meet them in public and the meeting was arranged. Not long into it he became terrified by the fanatical fury of the mullás and, realizing what a perilous situation he was in, chose to remain silent rather than venture into discussion.

The fear and panic provoked in him at the meeting emboldened the two clergy and soon after they placed posters along the streets and roadways of the district declaring the utter ignorance of the learned Bahá'í who came to debate them in public. As a result the populace grew mean and soon began mocking the Bahá'ís.

The Local Spiritual Assembly of Ṭihrán, in order to protect the members of the Bahá'í community, forbade them to debate or dispute with anyone in that district, but it was not long before the inflamed insolence of the arrogant clergy and the vile behaviour of the multitude reached an extreme. It was then that Fádil decided to confront the two mullás. Two other prominent Bahá'ís, Jináb-i-Mírzá Yúsuf Khán-i-Vojdání and Jináb-i- Aqá Mírzá 'Alí-Muḥammad-i-Sarreshteh-dár were willing to accompany him. The three agreed to inform no one of their plans so it would be clear to all that, should a dangerous situation with serious consequences result, responsibility for it was to be theirs and no one else's. Their next step was to request a meeting with the notorious clergy in order to plead a case for their beloved Faith. When he knew the response to their request was affirmative, Fádil drew up a list for his wife of all the monies owed him and then took steps to insure enough money was left in the house to cover all of his debts. He ate his lunch then

131

kissed his daughter Subhániyyih, bid farewell to his wife and departed his house to rendezvous with his two friends. The three walked resolutely into the Sangalaj district.

Meanwhile the two mullás had done their own kind of preparation. At the mosque they, arrogantly boasting of their own vastly superior knowledge, had announced to the people of the district, a vile section of the city's population surpassing all others in wickedness and depravity, the day and the hour that the Bahá'ís would come to converse with them. Thus prepared, the people anticipated with sanctimonious glee that the Bahá'ís would be defeated in the debate, sentenced by the mullás and left to them to be bodily torn apart by their own hands.

The Sangalaj streets, better described as alleys or lanes, were narrow, dirty and filled with gangs of chador-clad women standing around outside their houses. At first it seemed impossible to pass but slowly the three Bahá'ís made their way through the crowded alleys to arrive eventually at the house of Ḥájí Áqá Riḍá.

They entered the biruní, that outer part of the house considered to be for the men, and were ushered upstairs to a room already occupied by a group of men sitting on the floor. Among them Shaykh Muḥammad, brother of Áqá Riḍá who himself was still at the mosque, some tullábs, or theological students, several nondescript men and four armed policemen.

The three Bahá'ís made their entrance into the room and Fádil, because he was to be the spokesman,

132

was given a seat at the head of the room next to the specially cushioned place reserved for Ḥájí Áqá Riḍá. On the other side of it was seated his brother <u>Sh</u>ay<u>kh</u> Muḥammad. There were some formal exchanges, including the Muslim greeting, "Salám-Aleikum", then, to occupy the time before the arrival of Ḥájí Áqá Riḍá, discussion arose which revolved around the necessity of accepting the beliefs of the Athná Asharríyyih religion. This is a sect of Islám that believes in the Twelve Imáms and their legitimate and hereditary succession to the Prophet Muḥammad and in the claim that they were divinely inspired and endowed with all perfections. With <u>Sh</u>ay<u>kh</u> Muḥammad making some pointed assertions, which were clearly misinterpretations of the teachings of this sect, Fáḍil would, in turn, provide immediate repudiations, each of them quoting directly from the Muslim hadí<u>th</u> (traditions) and writings.

As his statements were one after another skilfully refuted by the artful words of Fáḍil, it soon became apparent to the <u>Sh</u>ay<u>kh</u> that he was rapidly losing ground in what he thought would be clear and decisive preliminary thrusts on his part. With a move of bravado he arose, and stepping into an adjoining room he soon reappeared laden with books and vainly imagining he was about to be vindicated by the unassailable evidence contained within them. What he, doubtless, expected would be reinforcement to support his statements, proved to be devastating ammunition against them. Fáḍil, using the same books, showed him citations, which repudiated each and all of his arguments.

The S͟haykh grew more intense. He was being humiliated in a discussion he had thought would bring glory to himself, vindication to Islám and defeat to his Bahá'í adversary. Inflamed, his voice became louder and its tone more violent and harsh. As he spoke, and while trying to emphasize a point to make it undeniably decisive, his head and body began to sway erratically and his hands gesticulate wildly. In the heat of it all, because the two were by then kneeling in order to face each other, the mullá's emphatic gestures moved him toward Fádil who, not failing to take note of the humorous aspect of what was happening, several times found himself advancing toward his adversary, to the extent that their knees were actually rubbing together.

Those who were witness to this scene watched and listened in amazement; the reaction of the four policemen, however, was astonishing and unexpected. Already the dignified bearing and luminous countenance of the shapely-turbaned Fádil had touched them. So much did their sympathies side with him that each time the S͟haykh's outbursts reached a peak and his tirades of impertinence and abuse rendered him incoherent, they would sympathetically take Fádil's side and attempt to stop or repress his assailant. This remarkable sequence of bombastic futility versus the dexterous use of a highly disciplined and spiritualised mind continued for more than an hour. The S͟haykh suffered defeat on each of the subjects he broached and was eventually saved from further ignominy in the eyes of the relatively small gathering by the arrival of his brother Ḥájí Áqá Riḍá who had just returned from the mosque.

As Áqá Riḍá entered the room all rose out of respect and, once he had seated himself, resumed their places ruminating, no doubt, over the possibilities of what might transpire next. After a moment of silence dense with expectation, Ḥájí Áqá Riḍá, who did not already know everyone in the room, turned in the direction of one familiar face and broke the silence with a few remarks on a theological subject. With that Fáḍil offered some pertinent comments on the same subject and it was then that the recently arrived mullá first noticed him. As a few formal courtesies were exchanged the same glint of recognition appeared in the eyes of each. Simultaneously the two realized that they had attended the same classes at the Theological Science Study Centre of the Ákhund Mullá Káẓím-i-Khurásání by the Holy Shrines in Karbilá, one of Islám's holiest cities in Iráq.

As one would expect, their discussion began around religious matters and it soon became clear that Ḥájí Áqá Riḍá, just as his brother had earlier, chose to focus his remarks around the need to accept and follow such religious beliefs as accorded with the mullá's own beliefs, interpretation and practice. Fáḍil, however, turned toward him and, gesturing with his hand from left to right spoke directly, "These questions you raise and those put forth by your honourable brother," he said, " have already been discussed, dealt with, and agreed upon to everyone's satisfaction." His eyes then searched those of the room's other occupants for a confirming response to what he had just

135

said. Indeed, nods of agreement were readily forthcoming, even from Shaykh Muḥammad.

Ḥájí Áqá Riḍá resorted then to raising a succession
of subjects and a strategy of using remarks and statements blatantly calculated to undermine Fáḍil's assertions and create suspicion and doubt in the minds of
those who were listening. Fáḍil however, in spite of all
the mullá's efforts, was able to demolish each of them
with an array of luminous proofs and brilliant arguments.

The debate continued several hours into the night
until finally Ḥájí Áqá Riḍá was reduced to silence and
his complete and utter defeat had become evident to
all present.

Fáḍil chose that moment to address the room of
witnesses saying, "Gentlemen, you have observed how
each and every question, objection and argument has
been answered, dealt with and refuted." To the brothers he said, "The logical inference of your silence
indicates that you have nothing more to say and, in
truth, that you have admitted defeat. Neither one of
you, therefore, has a right to say, in front of the people
at the mosque nor anywhere else, that the Bahá'ís are
afraid to come forward and debate with you."

There was an icy silence in the room for several
seconds, then Fáḍil rose to his feet along with his
companion Mírzá Yúsuf Khán-i-Vojdaní, (the other,
Mírzá 'Alí Muḥammad Khán-i-Sarreshtehdár, had left
the gathering earlier) and together they departed the
treacherous vespiary.

Soon after the occurrence of this significant event Fádil reported it to 'Abdu'l-Bahá and received the following Tablet in reply:

Ṭihrán

> Jináb-i-Fádil-i-Shírází, upon him be the glory of God, the All-Glorious!

> He is God!

> O thou who art firm in the Covenant! Thy letter was received. As time is lacking, a brief reply must be given—please forgive Me. Instructing the handmaidens of the Merciful in the home of Mírzá Isháq Khán will indeed be the cause of nearness to the threshold of the Blessed Beauty. I hope that thou shalt be assisted and confirmed therein.

> The gathering with the divines of Sangalaj and the presentation of luminous proofs and conclusive testimonies was a cause of great joy. My hope is that thou mayest ever continue to render service.

> The glory of glories rest upon Thee.

> Abdu'l-Bahá, Abbás
> 20 Jamádí (1) 1338 Haifa

Twenty-Seven

Hamadán

The year was 1919 when Fádil and his family, at the request of the Spiritual Assembly of Ṭihrán, moved to Hamadán where he and his wife took up posts teaching in the Ta'yíd and the Mawhibat schools which had both been started in 1913. 'Abdu'l-Bahá had encouraged Bahá'ís in Iranian cities to open schools following the stunning success of the Tarbiyat schools, one for boys and one for girls, in Ṭihrán. The family remained in Hamadán for three years. Besides their commitment to the schools, they established in their home a variety of evening activities for the Bahá'ís and seekers which included firesides, study classes and special courses designed to deepen the youth.

Although their stay in Hamadán had proven to be a very difficult one, Fádil never voiced a complaint. The only person with whom he would share his deepest feelings was 'Abdu'l-Bahá. In response to one of Fádil's letters to Him during the Hamadán period, 'Abdu'l-Bahá's most penetrating and moving explanation in the following Tablet strengthened Fádil and brought composure to his soul.

Jináb-i-Fádil-i-Shírází, upon him be the glory of God!

He is God!

O consummate scholar! Thy letter was received, but its contents were known in advance. Thou speakest the truth—it is indeed so. Yet that enthralling Beloved hath ever been wont to slay the lover and to set aflame the yearning heart. At one time He casteth him, Abraham-like, into a blazing fire; at another He confineth him to chains, as the truth-speaking Joseph. At one time, He maketh him, like unto Moses, a wanderer in the Midian desert and a homeless shepherd in mountains and fields. At another, He delivereth him, as the Chaste One (John the Baptist), to the oppression of the prideful Herod, and tingeth the earth with his blessed blood. And yet another time doth He expose his sacred breast to a thousand bullets of tyranny, like unto the Primal Point— He Who is the Mystery of Existence and the Manifestation of the Adored One, may My soul be a sacrifice unto Him.

Such are the ways and doings of that precious Beloved. But what recourse have we? The wound He inflicteth is a soothing balm and the poison He dispenseth but a healing remedy. "With somewhat of fear and hunger, and loss of wealth, and lives, and fruits, will we surely prove you: but bear good tidings to the patient."[15]

Wherefore be not grieved, but in adversity and prosperity alike be thou a partner and intimate associate of 'Abdu'l-Bahá. That which hath befallen Him hath now been visited upon thee. "And erelong shall God turn adversity into ease." Sorrow not, for verily God is with us. To proclaim the religion of God is at this juncture indeed a necessity, and to teach His Faith is incumbent upon us all.

Upon thee be greetings and praise.

'Abdu'l-Bahá, Abbás

Twenty-Eight

Return to Ṭihrán

Soon after the couple's return to Ṭihrán in 1922 Fádil resumed both his teaching at the Tarbiyat School and his activities within the Bahá'í community. In December of 1988 one of the oldest former students of Fádil shared with the writer his reminiscences of around this period of Fádil's life. Wishing to remain anonymous, he explains, "My state of mind regarding fame from the time I was a young man has been one of reluctance and without desire". Continuing he shares, "Now, at 82 years of age, I recall being a student of Jináb-i-Fádil-i-Shírází for a period of three years, around 1922-1925, at the Tarbiyat School for boys in Ṭihrán. There, Jináb-i-Fádil was teaching Persian literature and the Arabic language. I learned Arabic grammar and conjugation in his class and later on, for as long as I lived in Ṭihrán, which was over a period of six years, I attended his classes designed to deepen the younger generation of Bahá'ís in the teachings of the Faith and to train them in delivering effective Bahá'í speeches and in becoming accomplished speakers. I also attended his firesides at

141

different Bahá'í homes and benefited greatly from his presence.

"Of a few incidents that I still recall, one was at the time when some protestant Christian leaders or clergy were casting doubt and scepticism against Islám and attempting to arouse suspicion among the modern-minded people by saying that the Prophet Muḥammad was no holy man but that he was lascivious and many times married, thus trying to cause them to deviate, be driven backward and turn away from Islám.

"Jináb-i-Fáḍil, who at that time was the most learned and pre-eminent Bahá'í teacher inṬihrán, confronted the problem by devoting one of his weekly evening classes, designed for training the youth how to write and deliver essays on various Bahá'í topics, to address the issue. During the course of that evening he explained and enlarged upon the meaning of the Islámic hadith (tradition) regarding certain statements by Muḥammad in favour of women and talking of His love, His admiration and affection for them. By demonstrating convincing proofs and arguments he was able to cast aside any doubts and uncertainty that the Bahá'í youth might have entertained as a result of the protestant missionary's misguided attacks on the Prophet and to guard us from the suspicious and wavering young Muslims who were supporting those false claims.

Alas, after the passage of some 60 years since I heard Fáḍil's presentation on the subject, I am not able to recall the compelling proofs from the Qur'án and the Islámic traditions regarding the rights of women, both within the family and in the community, which he used to completely refute all the criticisms.

"The second instance that I remember regarding Jináb-i-Fádil is of an evening when I attended a fireside being conducted by him. There were three Muslim seekers present at the meeting. As I entered I greeted everyone in a loud and expressive voice saying, 'Alláh'u'Abhá! ('God is the Most Glorious', a Bahá'í greeting) to make clear I was a Bahá'í. I noticed that after my arrival the tone of Fádil's words gradually changed and tended to become harsh, which was unlike his usual conduct at his firesides. In a forceful and vehement voice he addressed those individuals saying, 'You keep repeating, our ulamá say this and our ulamá say that; well it's time you knew that we ourselves are considered ulamá!'

"Finally, after Jináb-i-Fádil's harsh toned words put an end to the protesting and objecting, the three men got up and left. Following their departure Fádil told the host and the two young Bahá'ís who had brought those men to the meeting that they were not after searching and investigating the Truth; rather their intention was to fuss, dispute and excite. 'I tried to show civility and condescension as I talked to them', he said, 'but as soon as I saw Jináb-i-..... enter the room and my eyes fell on his sword' (I was at that time an army officer and was wearing an army uniform) 'I had no more misgivings; in a frank and serious manner I responded to them. They got the message and left!'

"I said, 'Jináb-i-Fádil, I must admit that your harsh words probably scared me more than the three Muslims!'

"A third incident that I can remember is this: About the year 1309 H. (1930) there was an ákhund (Muslim theologian) by the name of Sharíat-i-Sangalají who had a school by the name of Dáru't-Tabligh-i-Islámí, meaning Islámic Propagation Centre. The school had a political thrust. Every Friday night the ákhund would go up the pulpit of the school and give a sermon. In his sermons he would implicitly make sarcastic remarks and derogatory insinuations about the Bahá'í Faith. As well as his students, on one particular occasion, there were several army officers, myself plus a few members of Parliament present for his talk.

"I would always share his remarks with other young Bahá'ís. Among those with whom I shared was my now deceased friend, 'Abdu'lláh Anvar. Together we would give an account of Sharíat's provocative hints to Jináb-i-Fádil. I remember how Fádil used two or three of his regular discussion gatherings, which took place on Friday afternoons at the Hazírat'ul-Quds of Tihrán (the Bahá'í National Centre), to indirectly respond to the erroneous remarks of Sharíat-i-Sangalají, often including lines from the famous poet Háfíz which always caused great excitement and enthusiasm among his listeners."

Twenty-Nine

More Reminiscences

Although there have been many instances over the years when the writer has heard distinguished individuals and former students of Tarbiyat school pay glowing tribute to their beloved teacher Jináb-i-Fádil-i-Shírází, yet it is one such student in particular I feel compelled to mention here, Jináb-i-Abú'l-Qásim Faizí, Hand of the Cause of God. According to my mother and grandmother, his love, admiration and respect for Fádil was so strong and deeply felt, that whenever he had occasion to speak of Tarbiyat school he would also pay homage to the two individuals towards whom he felt the greatest debt of gratitude; one of them was Jináb-i-Fádil-i-Shírází and the other was the school's principal, Jináb-i-Azíz'ulláh Messbáh. Their degree of sacrifice and service to the Cause had so intensely touched his heart and soul as to completely change his outlook on life and the direction his life would take. Often he would be heard to say, "I shall be forever indebted to them for all that I have."

Like Jináb-i-Abú'l-Qásim Faizí, other contemporaries of Fádil, those with whom he had close association and whose knowledge, erudition and scholarship earned them a prominent place as distinguished teachers of the Faith and servants of the Cause, have long since passed away. Those he taught and nurtured as his students over more than two decades some seventy to ninety years ago, have either passed on or are too old to recall stories they might have shared.

One who survives and has shared the following account is Dr. 'Izzatu'lláh Azízí, who resides in Vancouver, Canada. Dr. Azízí comes from a very distinguished Bahá'í family in Írán. His brother, Jalál Azízí, served on the National Spiritual Assembly and another brother, Eskandar, served on the Local Spiritual Assembly of Ṭihrán. Each, along with his cousin Habíbu'lláh Azízí, became martyrs of the Cause in 1981 and 1982. Mr. Azízí has given the following account:

"I was a student at the Tarbiyat School and knew Jináb-i-Fádil since my childhood. We studied the Qur'án in his class and at that early age we children could neither appreciate the value, rank and greatness of our teacher, nor were we capable of grasping the meanings of the revealed words of the Qur'án. Study of the Qur'án in Írán is compulsory at all schools and starts at the upper primary levels; consequently the children were noisy and disturbing. This would annoy and trouble Jináb-i-Fádil. We now realize how patient and forbearing this honoured and dignified soul must have been to endure all this while accepting a rather meagre salary to live on. Anyway, in 1925, when Jináb-i-Fádil and his family were living in a house owned by my father for a while until they could find a permanent place, he gave private lessons to my brothers and I.

"In 1927 I was 18 and planning to leave for France in order to continue my studies. I had decided to spend some of the summer months studying the Bahá'í writings such as the Kitáb-i-Aqdas, (the most Holy Book) the Kitáb-i-Íqán, (the Book of Certitude), and the Tablets to the Kings as well as certain difficult books in the Persian language. This would help me not only improve my knowledge of the Bahá'í writings but also in learning, to the extent possible, the Persian and Arabic languages. Therefore I asked Jináb-i-Fádil if he would agree that I come to him in his home in order to study those books. He was kind enough to accept my request so I began to take private classes regularly with him.

"His house, situated in one of the streets off Shaykh Hádí Avenue, now called 'Rází', was a small two bedroom home where Jináb-i-Fádil received me in a room which also served as his bedroom. His bedding would be rolled up in the daytime and put against the wall to serve as a cushion for leaning on as he was teaching. The second room belonged to his wife and two children, a girl and a boy. There was a courtyard with a small pond.

"It was in this modest house that this servant heard him expound on those Tablets. Even at that young age, it enabled me to become attracted by the greatness, majesty and grandeur of the Revelation. May his soul be blessed. With complete humility and submissiveness, deeply moved and with his face transformed, he would read from the Writings. It was as though he

147

had placed himself before God, bowing to pay homage to Him.

"One day he asked me, 'What is your purpose in going to Europe?'' To study,' I replied, 'I wish to become an engineer.'

"He greatly encouraged me saying you must certainly go and pursue the sciences that will enable you to achieve excellence so you can serve the Cause.'

"Then he confessed, 'When there is a gathering organized for the purpose of raising funds for the Cause and I am not able to participate you cannot imagine how much I suffer!' His words were so moving and so touched my heart that it has left a lifelong impression upon me. It was clear that he suffered for being deprived of the bounty of participating and serving the Faith through making such contributions.

"During that summer of 1927, while I was pursuing my classes, Jináb-i-Fádil seemed saddened and depressed. Apparently, his respected spouse, on the day of Áshurá, had been out to watch a procession of mourners. (This event refers to the 10th of Muharram, the 1st month in the lunar calendar of the Muslims on which occurred the great tragedy of Karbilá, the slaughter of the Prophet's grandson, Imám Husayn, His children and seventy heroic men who were in his company.) During this outing she had contracted something that caused her to experience a condition of discomfort. The condition worsened and eventually surgery was needed. It was obvious that due to financial constraints he was unable to cover such an unexpected expenditure. Now he had never asked me for any fees in exchange for the classes I was taking so this servant immediately asked if I might pay my dues for the lessons I was being given by him. In those days my late father was making payments for a construction project so I could not say anything to him but I mentioned it to my mother. Upon hearing me, my kind-hearted mother unhesitatingly opened her small metal chest and took out eight Tumán (Persian currency) and gave it to me. So I went to the house of my honoured professor and offered him the money. This eased his mind and brought him obvious content ment. It was clear that he was thankful to God.

"Since that time I have kept thinking that the higher in rank and station one is spiritually, the less he is given materially.

"May Jináb-i-Fádil forever be remembered and may peace and happiness be with his departed spirit".

Recalling that after Fádil had willingly given up all worldly possessions, status and title when he recognized Bahá'u'lláh, that he left his family and his native town and that his father had denied him his substantial inheritance, it may be of interest to note that Fádil's younger brother, Shaykh Muḥammad-Ḥusayn, after their father's death, came to visit Fádil in Ṭihrán. There he said, "This money belongs to you; let me purchase a house for you so that you and your family can live more comfortably." Such, however, was the degree of Fádil's detachment, that he refused.

In September of 1997, while attending the inauguration of the Shoghi Effendi Rabbání Chair in

Landegg Bahá'í Academy, Switzerland the writer heard
the following story from Mr. Hushmand Sábet:
"My mother, Tubá Khánum Sábet, had indicated in
her will that the sum of $9000 U.S. be paid to the
Universal House of Justice on behalf of each of her
three teachers, Jináb-i-Fádil-i-Shírází, Jináb-i-Fádil-i-
Mázandaráni and Hand of the Cause Jináb-i-'Alí-Akbar
Furutan. All of those sums were duly paid after her
death."

Of course Mrs. Sábet was fulfilling the Baha'i law of
inheritance according to which teachers are listed
among heirs because, according to Abdu'l-Bahá, a
teacher who is involved in the spiritual education of a
child is like a "spiritual father" who "endoweth his
child with everlasting life".[16]

Another distinguished Bahá'í who has shared with
the writer some of his childhood memories of Fádil's
later years is Dr. Iraj Ayman whose family were close
friends with Fádil and his family. He writes:

"The Fádil family at that time lived in a house that
belonged to my mother's uncle, Muhammad-Beik
Hamidí. Our house was very close to theirs so we went
over to their house nearly every day and had the good
fortune of visiting with Jináb-i-Fádil on an almost daily
basis; I have many memories of that time and will
share with you a few of them.

"To begin with I should point out that Jináb-i-
Shaykh Muhammad-Ibráhím Fádil-i-Shírází, in addition to being especially revered and respected within
the Bahá'í Community of Írán, was the object of a very
special love and affection of the beloved Guardian,
Shoghi Effendi. When, as a young man, Jináb-i-Qulám

Ḥusayn Farrokẖzád-i-Naráqí was leaving Írán to continue his graduate studies at the University of Beirut in Palestine he, because of the student-teacher relationship that had come to exist between him and Jináb-i-Fádil during the years he attended the Tarbiyat school for boys, he went to say goodbye to his teacher. On that occasion Fádil mentioned to him certain matters and asked that they be conveyed to Shoghi Effendi on his behalf when he would be having the honour of visiting him.

"Jináb-i-Farrokẖzád related to us some years later, 'After I came into the presence of the beloved Guardian, and in order to comply with Fádil's request, I began with, 'Jináb-i-Fádil-i-Shírází'; no sooner had I mentioned Fádil's name than the beloved Guardian repeated three times, 'Rúhí fidá' (may my life be a sacrifice for him). Notice how great was Jináb-i-Fádil's rank.

"Fádil taught at Tarbiyat School and had a very close relationship with Jináb-i-Mírzá 'Azízu'lláh Messbáh, who was then principal of the school. (Jináb-i-Messbáh was an outstanding literary composer, writer, author and poet.)

"Often seeing Jináb-i-Fádil I remember him as a devout and pious believer who was very much attracted to prayer and fasting and often found in a state of prayer and worship. He was also a very brave and courageous man; when confronted with dangerous situations in teaching the Faith he was fearless. The daring and bold manner by which he taught the Faith was a well-known fact amongst the Bahá'ís. He was willing to attend any meeting he was asked to even if

151

all present were ákhunds (Muslim clergy) who were enemies of the Cause and whose presence meant the danger of assault and attack on his life.

"Jináb-i-Fádil was a native of Da<u>sh</u>tistán in the southern part of Fárs Province (near the Persian Gulf) where there was a variety of seafood of which he was fond. His favourite was shrimp. Every year his relatives would send him dried salted shrimp and he was the only member of his family who would eat them.

"Every year some member of his brother's family, who was one of the ullamá of the Fárs Province, would come to Ṭihrán for a visit and would bring some of the specialties of that province such as dates and a particular sweet made out of dates and walnuts. (The writer would like to mention that as a child she remembers her grandmother preparing a desert dish made of dates, flour, butter and walnuts she called Ranginak and of it she would say, 'This is a recipe from your grandfather's native land.')

"Fádil's nephew, 'Alí Da<u>sh</u>tí, had been a newspaper editor, famous writer and senator of Írán. He was not a Bahá'í but was very devoted to Fádil and would come to visit him in the summer months. The Fádil family, in those days, would sleep in the courtyard by a small pool among some pomegranate trees. One night some armed thieves climbed the wall, entered the house and took some of their personal belongings. Since the chief of the criminal investigation department of the police headquarters was a Bahá'í by the name of Mr. Maḥmud Badí'í, the thieves were quickly found and arrested. But Jináb-i-Fádil interceded and asked that they be pardoned; he could not accept to see them punished and put in jail because of having inflicted damages to him.

"Fádil had a loud and expressive voice. Although, towards the end of his life he was weighed down with age, I recall nevertheless, that once when he was delivering speech without the use of a microphone at a meeting in the garden of the Bahá'í National Centre of Ṭihrán where over a thousand people had gathered, his voice could clearly be heard in all parts of that vast garden.

"I remember very well the day Jináb-i-Fádil passed away, and I remember his funeral. On the day of it, after I came home from school and heard the news, I ran to their house and we followed the crowd to the Bahá'í Cemetery called Gulistán-i-Jávíd (The Eternal Flower Garden) where a great crowd had gathered for the ceremony.

"The cemetery on the Khurásán Highway had been recently purchased and Jináb-i-Fádil had been one of the first Bahá'í's to be buried there. Later his son Abdu'lláh made a special design for his father's grave stone, a nine-pointed star within which the name Muḥammad Ibráhím Fádil-i-Shírází was engraved and under the star the dates of his birth and death were inscribed. It was the first gravestone to be designed and built in this unique fashion and everywhere among the believers there was talk about his gravestone. Until that time it had been the custom to cover gravestones with poems and writings. His gravestone remained there until 1979. (After the Islámic Revolution of 1979 Bahá'í cemeteries in Írán were

153

confiscated, the graves desecrated and the gravestones demolished by order of the Revolutionary Council).

"After the Tarbiyat school was closed by order of the Government Jináb-i-Fádil then occupied himself with teaching the Faith, conducting two separate deepenings, a writing class and two teacher training classes, one for men and the other for women.

"One of the devotees of Jináb-i-Fádil was a believer from Sangesar called Jináb-i-Alláh Qulí Subhání who had an expressive voice with a melodious tone and a deep knowledge of the Faith. He often accompanied Jináb-i-Fádil on his teaching trips and had many stories about the incidents that took place during those trips. One of them was the famous incident in Kurdistán (refer to next chapter) that he often talked about".

Thirty

The Kurdistán Incident

The ever present animosity toward the Bahá'ís as well as their persecution at the malevolent hands of the Islamic clergy and their entourage of fanatical followers did not deter Fádil and his wife from teaching the Faith. They were courageous in their willingness to bear afflictions and undergo trials and tribulations in order to enlighten those souls who were willing to listen and this, because they were convinced that only Bahá'u'lláh's teachings would unite the human race and safeguard the rights of its members regardless of race, creed or class. They were convinced that His teachings would promote personal freedom and initiative and give paramount importance to considering the welfare of others and that it would stress just dealings between communities, individuals and institutions. They believed that the application of His teachings was the thing needed in order for their country to progress and that, in the words of Bahá'u'lláh, "...the counsels the pen of this Wronged One hath revealed constitute the supreme animating power for the advancement of the world and the exaltation of its peoples."[17]

It was some time after their stay in Hamadán and subsequent return to the capital that the Local Spiritual Assembly of Ṭihrán was instructed by the beloved Guardian Shoghi Effendi to send a detached, staunch and well-informed Bahá'í teacher to the western province of Kurdistán. The Kurdish tribes who inhabit that province, which borders on Iráq and is mountainous for the most part, were a hardy nomadic people of the Sunní sect of Islám. When Fádil was chosen as the one to go he cheerfully accepted the assignment and soon set off for Kurdistán.

Once he had arrived and settled in he wasted no time contacting the ullamá of the region. Although they were known for their traditional orthodox views, during his encounters with them and despite their antagonistic and adversarial attitude, he presented decisive arguments and convincing proofs to answer their questions and make clear the truth of the Bahá'í teachings.

He also began a correspondence with the great Sunní leader Muláná Muḥammad, who, though replying to Fádil's letters, was not interested in meeting with him. Known among his Sunní followers for his vast store of knowledge he at length wrote to Fádil a wordy letter to say in effect, it had been divinely revealed to him that Fádil was not only far astray from the truth but in fact, an evil and misguided individual and that the cause he claimed to be true was, in reality, completely false.

Fádil's response to this was an eloquently worded letter in Arabic summoning to his argument Qur'ánic refutations of what the religious leader had written

156

and informing him that what he had expressed in his letter was in truth not God-inspired but the words and evil suggestions of Satan and that because of such a boldly presumptuous and wickedly perverse letter he would soon witness and be encircled by the swiftness, vehemence and fury of Divine wrath. What follows is a translation of Fádil's letter to the Sunní leader:

> In the name of God who chose to establish truth by His Words and to obliterate the uprooted blasphemers.
>
> Soon shall the Written Book be promulgated everywhere so that thy teacher shall know of knowledge and understanding. Verily, since thou hast chosen the way of darkness over the path of enlightenment, thy livelihood shall not prosper nor shall the tree of thy desire bear fruit; indeed thou shalt find thyself in evident loss. By God, he who turns away from God and His Verses hath not believed in God from all eternity to all eternity. By thy god, if what thou claimest is what thou believest, none but the devil, who inspires his followers, hath inspired thee and the lie thou dost utter issues from thine ego which hath deceived thee and those who follow thee. God is independent of thee and of all who are in the heavens and on the earth. How true that which Mawlaví Al-Rúmí hath said, "To denigrate the sun to me returneth that denigration, mine eyes are therefore blind and incapable of seeing." How strange it is that from one who claimest belief in Islám come

denigrating utterances worse than those which the unbelievers and detractors of the Qur'án have uttered! As God, blessed and glorified be He, hath said of such people, "And never came a Messenger to them but that they did mock him",[18] and, exalted be His utterance, "And when Our clear Verses are recited to them, they say, 'This (Muḥammad) is merely a man who would fain pervert you from your father's worship.'[19] And they say 'This (the Qur'án) is none other than a forged falsehood.'[20] And those who disbelieve say of the Truth when it has come to them, 'This is nothing but evident magic.'[21] Then sayeth He, praised and exalted be His utterance, 'And we sent not as Our Messengers before you (O Muḥammad) any but men to whom we gave Revelation. So ask if you know not, O you pagans of Meccá, of those who know the Scriptures (learned men of the Torah and the Gospel)."[22]

O Shaykh, worldly dominion hath occupied thee and deprived thee of the Lord of Mankind. The folly of thine own self-worship hath, without any proof, been thine inspiration. How well hath it been said in Persian, "The evil imaginings seen in thy dream and from which thou wert fleeing, were indeed of thine own making." God has inspired me by what He aforetime revealed to Muḥammad, upon him be the salutation of God, "Do not be grieved at their turning away from you. This is because they disbelieve in the Verses of God (the Qur'án)."[23] And further on, blessed and exalted be His Words, "Then if

they reject you (O Muḥammad) so were
Messengers rejected before you, who came
with Al-bayy'inal (clear signs, proofs, evidences)
and Scriptures and the Book."[24] And again He
sayeth, blessed and glorified be He, "And
when Our Verses (the Qur'án) are recited to
them they say, 'We have heard it (the Qur'án);
if we wish, we can utter the like; these are
nothing but ancient tales'."[25]

Know thou that we have not taken issue
with the Qur'án, but related for thee the
doings of those like thyself who, in past ages
turned away from God, so that thou mayest
know what was said before thee by those
whose hearts are like yours. Woe betide thee,
and them. Verily God shineth His light even
though the deniers shun it.

Fádil's prediction came to pass and indeed, within
three days Muláná Muḥammad fell suddenly ill and
died.

The story of this dramatic episode spread like
wildfire throughout the Bahá'í communities in Írán
provoking much discussion and causing thoughtful
individuals amongst the friends to wonder in awe at
its final outcome. The report of Fádil's teaching trip to
Kurdistán and his dealing with Muláná Muḥammad
was also conveyed to the beloved Guardian Shoghi
Effendi.

It is not clear how many communications took
place between Fádil and the Guardian. Apparently
Fádil's first correspondence with him was a letter

dated 3 Diy 1307 (24 December, 1927). Following is an extract of that letter:

"This humble servant, during my twenty five years of theological studies and research in Shíráz and Najaf, led an ascetic life in my search for truth and undertook painstaking practices, exertions and struggles the like of which has never been seen or heard in past ages. As a result I attained such an exalted condition as to be able to discover and witness unimaginable realities. My earnest search eventually led me to the discovery, recognition and certitude of the truth of this Great Cause without the intermediary of any teacher save the Divine. In the year 1320AH (1903) I traveled on foot from Najaf to the Holy Land and attained the presence of my Lord, His Holiness Abdu'l-Bahá. During my sojourn in Akká I also had the great honour of meeting you...." He then goes on to give Shoghi Effendi some account of his life story up to that time.

Any correspondence he may have received from Shoghi Effendi through his secretary would have been among Fádil's personal papers and books which had to be carefully hidden in an undisclosed place by his younger daughter Rúháníyyih during the 1979 Islámic Revolution in Írán. She was the only family member who, along with her husband and their children, was still living there at that time. His older daughter Subháníyyih, who had pioneered with her family to Switzerland in 1956 and who passed away there in 1997, was in possession of a copy of a letter Shoghi Effendi had written through his secretary, Jináb-i-Zarqání, dated 23 Jamádiyu'th-tháni, 1345 AH (1927) which acknowledges receipt of Fádil's translation, earlier forwarded to the Guardian, of the Kitáb-i-Aqdas into Persian (from Arabic), and adds that he is fondly remembered and that his name is frequently mentioned by the beloved Guardian.

Thirty-One

The End of a Journey

Fádil's services to the Cause continued, of course, after his return to Ṭihrán from Kurdistán. But in spite of his role as teacher at the Tarbiyat School, in spite of his nightly firesides, his numerous study classes in which he answered for the believers their most intricate questions and resolved their most challenging issues, the depth of his knowledge, wisdom and learning remained, for the most part, unknown to the friends.

The renown Bahá'í scholar and writer, Jináb-i-'Azízu'lláh Sulaymání authored, in several volumes, a great biographical work known as Maṣábíh-i-Hidáyat, (Lamps of Guidance); it covers the life and work of a series of learned and distinguished Bahá'ís known for, among other things, their great erudition. In the first volume the author has dedicated a portion to Fádil-i-Shírází and in the opening paragraph of it he states, "This great and learned scholar and mystic sage, who spent 45 years of his precious life in service to the Cause of God, was not befittingly recognized or utilized, for although he had a profound mastery of the Qur'án and of Islámic traditions, he was also an expert in theosophy, a variety of philosophical arts and had reached the sublime and noble heights of mysticism. Yet most of his time was spent teaching Arabic at an introductory level to young students at the Tarbíyat Bahá'í School. Persevering with patience, fortitude and forbearance, Jináb-i-Fádil thus became an unintentional means of proving the saying, 'Hassanát-il-Abrár sayyíát-il-Muqarrabíne', (The good deeds of the righteous are the sins of the near ones)." Towards the end of the biography the author added a regretful note, "Neither had Fádil's vast knowledge been sufficiently appreciated and utilized nor was he adequately respected and revered; with the exception of a few knowledgeable and learned believers, no one understood the scope of his knowledge nor the depth of his faith."

Fádil, nevertheless, passed his days with patience and fortitude, equanimity, meekness and forbearance until the year 92 of the Bahá'í Era (1935). That year on the day of Naw-Rúz (Bahá'í New Year) when he gave presents to his children he told them, " This is my last Naw-Rúz with you; next year it will be your mother you will receive your gifts from."

The following month, on the occasion of the 9th day of the Ridván Festival, at the Hazírat'ul Quds (the National Bahá'í Center) in Țihrán, he delivered a two hour long address which was to be his last. After returning home from the meeting a high fever developed and he was confined to his bed. Although the illness prolonged over more than four months, during that time he would, in an exalted state of complete joy, engage in discussions with the believers who came to visit.

Towards the end, as the number of visitors increased and the visits became more frequent, his doctors became alarmed. Aware the situation had become harmful to his condition they would tell visitors, "If you love Jináb-i-Fádil, do not trouble him like this." Although these words were inscribed on a blackboard outside his room Fádil, when he became aware of it, asked that the words be erased and the friends permitted to visit.

His last physician, an eminent Bahá'í named Dr.'Abdu'l-Karím Ayádí, continued till the end, to check on him twice a day and members of the National Spiritual Assembly of the Bahá'ís of Írán would take turns coming to visit each night.

On the eve of Thursday the 27th of Shahrívar of the year 1314 (August 1935) Fádil told Naw-Zuhúr that in a few hours he would be gone from this world, advised her on matters of their three children then gave her instructions to be patient and to surrender her will to God's. Calling for his children he embraced each one of them and kissing them on their cheeks, dismissed them to their beds. Often during his illness he would ask his daughter Subháníyyih, who had a very beautiful chanting voice, to chant for him his favourite Tablet from 'Abdu'l-Bahá. Once more, on his final evening and at his request, she chanted it for him for the last time. The translated text of that Tablet is as follows:

He is God!

O My God, and My Beloved, and My Desire, and the Object of Mine adoration!

Verily Thy true servants have hastened unto that spring which welleth in the all-highest Paradise and quaffed from this abundant source the streams of Thy knowledge and the waters of Thy bounty. Thus by Thy grace hath the spirit of life pervaded their inmost realities, even as the soft breezes that waft over the meads and the gentle winds that blow through the woods.

Amongst them is this servant of Thine, upon whom Thou hast shone the light of guidance from Thy supreme Horizon, to whom Thou hast granted the full measure of Thy favours, and whose cup Thou hast made to brim over with the wine of Thy love. Thou hast singled him out to exalt Thy word, to diffuse Thy fragrances, and to raise Thy call amidst Thy creatures, that every attentive ear may hear Thy supreme glad-tidings. Praise be to Thee for what Thou hast brought forth in Thy grace and generosity, and thanks be to Thee for what Thou hast bestowed and conferred through Thy favour and bounty.

O God, My God! Do Thou ordain for this Thy servant that which Thou hast ordained for 'Abdu'l-Bahá, and grant that he may offer up his soul in the field of sacrifice in Thy path, O Lord of Grandeur. Thou, verily, art He Who remaineth true to His word, He Who excelleth

in His grace, and Thou, verily, art the Most
Generous, the All-Bountiful.

'Abdu'l-Bahá, Abbás

Finally, around midnight, as he lay in his bed and,
in spite of his weak condition, he recited the Long
Obligatory Prayer, making signs to indicate each
prescribed movement. At 1:30 a.m., with his body in
peaceful repose, his radiant and stalwart spirit took its
flight to the kingdom of glory and the world of delight. He was seventy-two years of age.

***

Within a few hours after the news of Fádil's passing
had been disseminated, a huge crowd gathered outside
his home to pay their respects. Next afternoon when
the funeral service took place the same crowds and
more, joined the procession to Gulistán-i-Jávíd.

The following account has been given by Jináb-i-
Áqá Ghulám Husayn Keyván, a devoted believer and
distinguished teacher of the Faith, also an intimate
friend of Jináb-i-Fádil: "When I was going on
pilgrimage to the house of the Báb in Shíráz, Jináb-i-
Fádil asked me to look up the resting place of the
dervish, 'Abdu'l-Hamid, and there to offer prayers that
the pure spirit of that inspired mystic who guided
Fádil in his search for truth and for whom he bore
great affection, would aid me in acquiring
magnanimity. Finding the grave in Shíráz I fulfilled
Fádil's request before returning to Tihrán.

"During the period of time when Fádil was sick and confined to bed I visited him every day. One night in a dream I saw someone giving me an envelope; it looked like the sort that would contain a telegram. Where the sender's address is usually indicated, the following phrase was written, 'As Sáhat-i-Kibriá', (From the Court of the Almighty). Instantly I wanted to open the envelope to read its contents. It was then I awoke.

"For two or three minutes I pondered the dream and then a shadow appeared at the head of my bed. It slowly moved down until it reached the bottom of it then turned...a face appeared and it was then I could hear a clear voice say, 'Come quickly!', then it vanished. This experience caused me to wonder, 'Perhaps I am going to die!'

"The next morning I went to see Fádil and told him of the dream and what I had seen after I woke up. He said this is a wonderful dream but I am not going to explain its interpretation until it comes to pass. A few days later his condition worsened and he told me the dream referred to him and that he was about to go. When I returned to see him that evening and saw the sign of death on his forehead I kissed it as a sign of bidding him farewell then left and returned home. At dawn they brought me the news that Fádil had ascended."

Nine days after Fádil's passing a telegram in English was received by the National Spiritual Assembly from the beloved Guardian, Shoghi Effendi and was translated and distributed; its content is as follows:

"The passing of the beloved and well known teacher (Fádil-i-Shírází) has caused me deep and profound sorrow. His services are forever immortalized. Reassure his family of my affection and loving prayers, Shoghi."

Fádil was survived by his wife Naw-Zuhúr Khánum, his son 'Abdu'lláh, and his daughters Subháníyyih, (the writer's mother) and Rúháníyyih.

Among Fádil's writings and literary works left behind was found an 'estedlálíyyih-i-ilmí', a book of scientific and methodical arguments compiled according to philosophical terms and idioms. Also found was an unfinished book on the art of logic. As well, there were several treatises and dissertations he wrote in response to those who opposed and criticized the Faith, one of which answered the objections and criticisms of a well known mujtahid by the name of Muḥammad-i-Khálessizádeh. In addition, was a treatise comprised of his discussions with Jamál-i-Burújirdí in Qum while visiting the tomb of Mírzáy-i-Qumí. This he wrote in refutation and repudiation of the Covenant breakers and sent a copy of it to 'Abdu'l-Bahá. The Master sent instructions for him to distribute it among the believers; in compliance Fádil printed many copies for distribution among the Bahá'ís.

Although Jamál-i-Burújirdí, to whom Bahá'u'lláh gave the title, 'Ismu'lláhu'd-Jamál (The Name of God, Jamál), remained foremost among the teachers of the Faith for several decades, he was nevertheless a proud, ambitious and arrogant believer and after the ascension of Bahá'u'lláh, along with others who broke the Covenant, was led astray and finally perished. (For a more complete account of him and other Covenant breakers see, "The Revelation of Bahá'u'lláh", by Adíb Táhirzádeh).

Because of his extreme sense of detachment and humility Fádil, according to his daughter Subháníyyih, never wanted to keep his writings, among which were a number of song lyrics and poetry. "My mother," she would say, "was often seen taking torn pieces of paper belonging to my father out of the waste basket, attempting to salvage what she could of his writings for herself."

APPENDIX

Among the personal papers of Fádil's spouse, Naw-Zuhúr Khánum, was found a notebook in which she had written a brief account of the life of Fá'izih Khánum, the beloved aunt who took care of her and her sister when they had become orphaned; on the cover of the handmade notebook is the following inscription written in Naw-Zuhúr's own handwriting:

"Although this lowly and insignificant handmaid of the threshold of the Blessed Beauty, Bahá'u'lláh, considers herself unworthy of any mention, she nevertheless finds it necessary to put into writing what she can remember about the heroic life of her dearest aunt, the late Fá'izih Khánum. Perchance, while reading this brief account about her and her husband, the late Áqá Siyyíd Ṣádiq, this unworthy and evanescent maidservant will also be remembered."

What follows is Naw-Zuhúr's tribute to her aunt combined with additional information the writer was able to obtain from other sources.[26]

170

Fá'izih Khánum, The Heroine

In the year 1272 A.H. (1855 A.D.) a daughter was born to a notable and respected family in Iṣfahán and was named Gulsurkh Bagum. Her other given name was Fátímih-Sultán Bagum. Her father, Áqá Mírzá Muḥammad-Ḥusayn, a descendant of the Imáms and one of the distinguished ulamá of Iṣfahan, was already at an advanced age when his daughter was born. He had been among the divines of that city who, in the year 1262 A.H. (1846) attained the presence of the Báb. It happened during the Báb's sojourn in the house of the Imám Jum'ih, the principal ecclesiastical dignitary of Iṣfahán.

The Báb's fame had spread over the entire city and had brought crowds of curious visitors to the house of the Imám Jum'ih. But it was not curiosity that drew the ecclesiastical authorities; they came with clear intentions of challenging the validity of the Báb's claim. Mírzá Muḥammad-Ḥusayn, however, upon meeting and conversing with the Báb and hearing Him reveal and recite Divine Verses with force and courage, became greatly enamoured of Him and for the rest of his life harboured for the Báb a deep love and devotion.

Many years later, as his daughter was growing up, he shared with her this account of his memorable visit with the Báb:

"I attained the presence of that Great One at the house of the Imám Jum'ih and there beheld a youth whose face was most luminous. I presented Him with twelve questions; He answered most of them clearly and eloquently and of the others He remained silent. The power and majesty with which He spoke confounded me; I am convinced He is the promised Qá'ím and I am fed up and disgusted with all the accusations and sneers with which His followers are afflicted. Furthermore I am pained and tormented over the unjust and cruel martyrdom of the Nurayn-i-Nayerane, (The Twin Shining Lights)".

Áqá Muḥammad-Ḥusayn was here refering to two honorable and distinguished Bahá'í brothers, descendants of the House of the Prophet Muḥammad. By profession they had been merchants in Iṣfahán and were highly esteemed and respected by every one for their rare integrity of character and honesty in their business transactions.

The Imám Jum'ih, who was the highest ecclesiastical authority of Iṣfahán, owed the brothers a large sum of money and wickedly schemed to have them imprisoned. Rather than pay off his debt he denounced them as Bábís, had them imprisoned and demanded of Zillu's-Sulṭan, the Governor, that he excecute them. At length, they were brought out of prison in chains, decapitated and with ropes fastened to their legs, their bodies were dragged to the great public square and left to be desecrated by the mob.

172

The bloodthirsty mob sacked their beautiful residences; the ornaments, even the flowers and trees of the gardens surrounding their homes were either taken or destroyed. 'Abdu'l-Bahá has since elevated their rank by titling them, "King of the Martyrs" and, "Beloved of the Martyrs".

Mírzá Muḥammad-Ḥusayn had recognized the Báb and accepted His claims but decided to conceal his belief due to the great turmoil that the Báb's stay in Iṣfahán had aroused. As His popularity grew, the degree of hostility and hatred demonstrated towards Him by the ecclesiastical authorities of that city was such that, to undermine His claims and character, some of the ulamá openly engaged in spreading false accusations and making slanderous remarks, even from the pulpit.

When, at length, Mírzá Muḥammad learned of the martyrdom of the Báb his grief and sadness knew no bounds. Later, when news reached him of the cruel killing of the two brothers, who were residents of his own native city, he was utterly disconsolate and for days and nights lamented, repeating over and over, "They have martyred the two great pillars".

In early womanhood Gulsurkh Bagum, was mature, intelligent and capable. She married her cousin Áqá Siyyid Ṣádiq, a talented artist and designer and a skilled carver. When he decided to move to Ṭihrán, the capital, where he knew there would be a greater market for his art, he expected his wife to go with him. Gulsurkh Bagum, however, chose to stay and look after her old father, who by then was over 100 years old. He, on the other hand, was eager to see his

daughter go to Ţihrán, for he had heard that the
prophecies of the Báb concerning the Rij'at-i-Ḥusayní,
prophecies relating to a belief held by the Shi'ah sect
of Islám dealing with the return, or advent of the
Imám Ḥusayn following the coming of the Qá'ím, had
already taken place.

One day, in private, the old man said to his
daughter, "Do you not want to go to Ţihrán to
discover God's hidden mystery? The Qá'ím, whose
advent you are waiting for, was none other than the
youth from Shíráz whose presence I attained. Now
that the Rij'at (Return) has taken place and I am too
old to go searching for Him, will you not undertake to
investigate and let me know too?"

Gulsurkh Bagum reassured her father that, when
the time was right, she would search for the Promised
One until she found Him.

After her father passed away she was free to leave
Iṣfahán, join her husband in Ţihrán and begin her
search. It was something of an advantage for her to
have grown up in a family of very accomplished and
competent theologians; while doing so she had been
able to gain a good grasp of Islámic teachings and
beliefs, a rare thing for a Persian woman of that time.

With an open mind and an eager spirit Gulsurkh
Bagum began her search. Of great assistance in her
undertaking was finding out that one of her brothers,
Siyyid Mihdí, was residing in Ţihrán and had already
embraced the Bahá'í Faith. She studied with him,
declared her faith in Bahá'u'lláh and from then on,
shining like a radiant flame of fire, she became an
intoxicated lover of the Blessed Beauty, Bahá'u'lláh.

In her autobiography, explaining about her nature and character before she became a Bahá'í she states, "In those days, because of ignorance, I was full of pride, as if God had not created anyone else but me. Because of my extreme haughtiness I never greeted anyone or showed modesty or humility towards anyone, not even my husband."

But when her heart became illumined with the light of faith and recognition she was recreated and her life was changed completely. She became immersed in the study of the Verses and Tablets and was constantly in the service of the friends, helping and assisting anyone in need.

Having discovered the Faith, a gem of inestimable value, she wished, in utmost humility, to offer it to her husband but he would not accept. According to Islámic law he believed it to be unlawful to associate with his wife who, as far as he was concerned, had renounced her faith. He was even against allowing her to live with him.

Distinguished Bahá'í teachers whom that pious and faithful handmaid would, out of love, invite to their home to meet her husband and answer his questions face to face, were unable to remove his deep seated hatred toward the Faith. Their efforts could neither end his antipathy for her nor prevent him from causing her a great deal of pain and suffering.

In return Gulsurkh Bagum persevered in showing kindness, humility and submissiveness towards her husband even when, on one occasion, out of exasperation, he would raise his hand as if to strike her. This zealous woman who, before her declaration, would have never accepted such a disgrace, would now take his hand and kissing it say, "God's instruction is to kiss the hand of the executioner".

This behaviour affected her husband profoundly and caused him to ponder and deeply reflect upon it. That night in a dream he saw a beautiful bird with a long beak sitting on a rooftop and chanting a verse from the Qur'án: "Did I not command you, O Children of Adam, that you should not worship Shaytán (Satan). Verily, he is a plain enemy to you; and that you should worship Me (referring to Alláh the Creator). That is the straight path".[27] Áqá Siyyid Ṣádiq awoke and, while turning the dream over in his mind, fell asleep again, and again saw the bird which chanted the same verse. The vision was repeated three times that night, each time adding to his amazement and giving rise to wonder.

That morning in an unprecedented attitude of kindness he called his wife to him and, holding an envelope in one hand and a box in the other, he addressed her in a friendly manner saying, "I have prepared a letter containing certain questions which I have placed in this box and locked. This envelope contains a white sheet of paper which I want you to send to your Master, 'Abdu'l-Bahá."

Gulsurkh Bagum accepted the task and sent the plain letter.

Upon receiving 'Abdu'l-Bahá's reply, answers corresponding exactly to the questions of which only he himself was aware, Áqá Siyyid Ṣádiq wholeheartedly embraced the Faith and, asking the forgiveness of his wife, he apologized to her for his past behavior.

176

From then on he accepted and approved of all her Bahá'í service and activities and left her completely free to teach and serve the Faith, even allowing her to appear in meetings and gatherings without a veil. She then, joyously and with great enthusiasm, committed herself to the service of her Lord.

Sometime later Siyyid Ṣádiq was honoured with a Tablet from 'Abdu'l-Bahá in which it was pointed out to him that never until then had an individual asked the servant of the servants (i.e.'Abdu'l-Bahá) questions with the intention of testing by receiving the answers and that it is not for man to test God. The Tablet then explained to Siyyid Ṣádiq that it was because of the persecution, the painstaking efforts and suffering that his wife had endured in promoting the Cause, her high endeavours in serving the captives and prisoners and her steadfast and staunch faith while facing the severe opposition and taunts of the Faith's enemies, that his questions had been answered.

In the same Tablet 'Abdu'l-Bahá invited the couple to make their pilgrimage to 'Akká to visit the shrine of Bahá'u'lláh. Elated over this, they were soon making preparations to travel.

Because their journey was to be undertaken at a time when activities of the violators of the Covenant were at their peak and it had become very difficult for pilgrims to reach their destination, the couple took the direction of Mecca and Bádkubih (a city in Russian Ádharbáyján) in order to reach 'Akká safely. Once there, abundant blessings, bestowals and favours of 'Abdu'l-Bahá were showered upon them. It was then that 'Abdu'l-Bahá named her "Fá'izih" (she who has attained). During the pilgrimage 'Abdu'l-Bahá assured Fá'izih that her father had, in fact, passed on to the next world a believer.

At the time of their departure, having sojourned several months in 'Akká, they were summoned to the presence of 'Abdu'l-Bahá Who, after offering them His love, affection and giving them exhortations said to Siyyid Ṣádiq, "I have bestowed upon your wife the title of Fá'izih so that she would dedicate her life to teaching and the service of the Faith; you must assist her." From then on she was known and addressed by the Bahá'ís as Fá'izih Khánum.

According to the Master's instructions the couple, upon their return home, rededicated their lives to teaching the Faith and diffusing the divine fragrances. Now, with even more enthusiasm and ardour than before, they committed themselves to carrying out the Master's wishes.

Fá'izih Khánum's association with high society and aristocratic families in Ṭihrán led her to cultivate close friendships with many of the upper class ladies. This allowed for opportunities to teach them about the Faith and, as a result, some became believers.

She was many times granted an audience by various dignitaries. During an uprising resulting in the imprisonment of fellow Bahá'ís, Fá'izih Khánum sent a petition to His Majesty Muẓaffari'd-Dín Sháh on their behalf and, with a number of ladies of influential background, pleaded to the Judicial Council for justice. While defending the prisoners she was able to visit them in prison, give them encouragement and bring them food, clothing, news and progress reports on her activities for their release.

It was during the imprisonment of Hand of the Cause Jináb-i-Ibn-i-Abhar by the order of Prince Kámrán Mírzá, the Náyibu's Salṭanih (Viceroy) and third son of Náṣiri'd-Dín Sháh, that she served Jináb-i-Ibn-i-Abhar like a sister and played a great part in bringing about his release from prison. She was also, by using a variety of means and by going through different agencies, able to repel and get rid of street ruffians who were out to harm and torture the Bahá'ís.

Along with these most laudable activities Fá'izih Khánum would host gatherings in her home, regular classes designed to train the believers how to teach the Faith. In all her activities and services for the Faith she was supported by 'Abdu'l-Bahá with abundant praise and warm encouragement

Now it was obvious that a woman of her stature, so brave, outspoken, and known to be a Bahá'í, would have many enemies among the clergy and their fanatical supporters who were ever waiting for an opportunity to attack and do murderous violence to her. Finally a chance to fulfill their bloodthirsty desires arrived.

Late one afternoon the tall and slender Fá'izih Khánum, wrapped in her black chádur (a large veil worn by women to cover their body and dress) was returning home from a meeting. Her thirteen-year-old niece Olfatíyyih and her maid, who walked behind them carrying some Bahá'í books under her chádur, accompanied her. As they approached the Bágh-i-

179

Firdaws district in which they resided they heard the voice of a child in distress calling loudly, "Fá'izih Khánum, please come and help me; these kids are going to kill me!" As the kind lady moved toward the children intent upon dispersing them and rescuing the distressed child, a cruel and obstinate enemy, who for some time had been longing for an opportunity to put an end to the brave woman, recognized her and called out to his murderous cronies, "Lets go! Here's our chance to wipe out the Fátimih Zahrá of the Bahá'ís!" ("Fátimih Zahrá", is a reference to the daughter of the Prophet Muhammad, wife of the Imám 'Alí and the highest-ranking woman of the Islámic dispensation).

As soon as his hooligan friends heard him, each grabbed whatever weapon they could find at hand, whether a rock, stick or knife, and rushed maliciously towards her. Fá'izih Khánum, realizing that she had fallen into their wicked trap, signalled the two younger women to run. As the frightened pair began to distance themselves from her she began to run also but the attackers, catching up, assailed her with blows, knocked her to the ground and, as she was driven under their feet, kicked her mercilessly.

In the meantime her niece, terrified and crying, ran towards the house of Náyib Husayn, the district's Police Deputy who, because of Fá'izih Khánum's continued display of care and amiability towards him had grown friendly toward and ready to assist the Bahá'ís. When the fearful young girl arrived Náyib Husayn was not around but his mother, who was in her room performing her evening prayer, responded to Olfatíyyih's plea for help and, breaking off her prayer, rushed out to find her son. As soon as he was informed of the situation, the strong, and robust man grabbed his silver headed club and made for the scene. Arriving in time, he beat the attackers to the ground, pulled Fá'izih's half dead body from under their feet and sent them fleeing in terror to escape the fury of his club. Assuredly, through his intervention, he also prevented the attackers from pillaging the victim's house and burning it down once they had succeeded in beating their victim to death.

Because of the injuries and broken bones she suffered, Fá'izih <u>Kh</u>ánum was bedridden for four months and lost the sight of an eye that had been brutally smashed. But her amazingly heroic attitude toward that incident long after it ended was evident in the frequent practice she made of reminding her niece that she had deprived her aunt of the gift of martyrdom.

As a result of this calamitous incident the Beloved Master revealed, in her honour, eloquent and jewel-like words of praise and commendation, applauding her and extolling her for the tragic hardship and afflictions she had borne for the sake of the Blessed Beauty. The same Tablet foretells that Áqá Siyyid Ṣádiq would also bear anguish, be inflicted by blows and suffer the slander of his enemies. Although it did come to pass, it served only to fuel the ardour and fire the enthusiasm of the faithful couple to continue, with complete steadfastness, to devote themselves entirely to the service of the Cause.

During the early nineteen hundreds, under the instructions of 'Abdu'l-Bahá, construction had begun on the first Ma<u>sh</u>riqu'l-A<u>dh</u>kár (House of Worship) of the Bahá'í World in the city of I<u>sh</u>qábád in Russian Turkistán. Many believers in the East were eager to dedicate their resources toward it. This included Áqá Siyyid Ṣádiq and his spouse whose great longing had been to consecrate all their material possessions to their beloved Cause. The construction project offered them an opportunity to realize their heart's desire. During their sojourn in 'Akká they had many times begged the Beloved Master to approve their resolve to liquidate all their properties and belongings and forward the funds to Him to be expended in God's path. Finally after their repeated supplications He, through a special Tablet revealed for them, conveyed His approval telling them that until then He had never accepted such offers from any one but since they had besought Him repeatedly, He would, therefore, accept.

It was when 'Abdu'l-Bahá's call to the believers to support the Temple Fund was received that the faithful and devoted couple at once set about to sell their home and all its furnishings and send the funds to I<u>sh</u>qábád for the construction of the Temple. After informing 'Abdu'l-Bahá of their action He revealed a Tablet in their honour praising them for the sacrifice they had performed, saying that this was indeed a lofty endeavour which has certainly been accepted before the Threshold of Oneness and that their exemplary sacrifice was the cause of joy and happiness to Him.

Fá'izih <u>Kh</u>ánum attained the presence of the Master a second time, then in the company of Hand of the Cause, Jináb-i-Ibn-i-Abhar. Upon returning home, in obedience to the instructions of 'Abdu'l-Bahá, she traveled to various parts of Írán to teach and proclaim the Faith. Although during this time enemies of the Faith made many attempts on her life she was enabled to escape each time, through divine intervention.

Some time after his passing a biographical sketch of the late Siyyid Ṣádiq appeared, along with an illustration, in the Persian section of Star of the West's March 2, 1915 issue. The article begins by giving a brief account of his lineage as a Siyyid and traces it back twenty eight generations to Imám Ja'far Ṣádiq, the 6th Imám of the Shi'ah sect of Islám. Mentioning that he passed away as the result of a heart attack at the age of eighty-two the article said of him that, "He was an artist by profession and that many of his works could be found in the United States. "His spirit," the article said, "like a bird from its earth-bound cage, took its flight from this transitory life to its freedom in the heavenly kingdom", and added, "His spouse, who is also his cousin, the daughter of the late Áqá Mírzá Ḥusayn-i-Mujtahid of Iṣfahán is the saintly and respected leaf, Fá'izih Khánum, that devoted and zealous teacher of the Cause.

"After 19 years of service to the Faith he sent two letters to 'Abdu'l-Bahá expressing the wish that he would be allowed to leave this transient world under the shadow of the Covenant lest his faith be shaken by tests and trials. A Tablet came in which he received the glad tidings of his approaching flight to the immortal kingdom. Thus for his two final months, when meeting with Bahá'ís and non Bahá'ís, he would tell them that he was soon to die of a heart attack. Last

year some Rawḍih Khán (professional narrators re-
citing the tragedies of Karbilá and the sufferings of the
House of the Prophet) had used the pulpit within his
own caravanserai to try to disgrace him with bad and
abusive language but 'Abdu'l-Bahá, in a Tablet, con-
soled and comforted him. Again in the month of
Ramadán (the Muslim month of fasting) in the Sháh's
mosque he quarrelled with someone who was making
insulting and slanderous remarks toward the Faith, to
the point where the crowd pushed forward to attack
and kill him. Fortunately a number of believers
present were able to come to his rescue and help him
escape.

"The couple did not have any children of their own
but they had raised several orphans from babyhood
and put them through school. These children all have
held jobs in various governmental offices.

"He was a very respected man, tall and well-
mannered. With his last breath he said, 'O 'Abdu'l-
Bahá, release me.' Praise be to God that he attained to
his utmost desire."

Immediately following the article, Star of the West
published two of the Master's Tablets revealed in
honour of the couple after they had sold their home
and belongings and sent the proceeds to the Ishqábád
Temple Fund.

Fá'izih Khánum's services and sacrifices continued
for fifteen years after the death of her husband and,
although that lowly maidservant of God had become
old and frail, she never neglected the teaching work
nor to help and assist the needy whether friend or
stranger; nor did she forsake the pursuit of her interest

184

in putting children through school, all of which made her the recipient of her Lord's abundant favours and bestowals.

Now and then she sent elegies and odes to 'Abdu'l-Bahá and He would, in turn, admire and praise her and tell her that her selfless and tireless service in the path of God has won the good pleasure of her Lord, adding, "Fá'izih is indeed firm in the Covenant".

There are many stories that demonstrate Fá'izih Khánum's loyalty to the Covenant; the following is one of them:

Among the leading teachers of the Faith during the time of Bahá'u'lláh was a man known as Jamál-i-Burújirdí entitled, by Bahá'u'lláh, Ismu'lláh u'l-Jamál (the Name of God, Jamál). He was respected and revered among the Bahá'ís for his vast knowledge but he was ambitious and had a lust for leadership. For many years he was able to hide his true character and feelings. Finally in the early years of the ministry of 'Abdu'l-Bahá, Jamál-i-Burujirdí, siding with the claims of the rebellious Mírzá Muḥammad-Alí, broke the Covenant and was expelled from the Faith.

Now for some years while Jamál-i-Burújirdí lived in Ṭihrán Fá'izih Khánum was one of his friends and would often consult with him over her affairs and engagements. But when he violated the Covenant Fá'izih Khánum arose out of the test's crucible like pure gold, distancing herself from him and referring to him in her writings as 'peer-i-kaftár' (the old hyena)!

She suffered from the activities of the Covenant breakers but with utmost faith and conviction held fast to the Covenant and Testament. In the year

1346 A.H. (1929) when, at the age of seventy-four she passed away in Ṭihrán, she was in a state of complete certitude. Those close to her at the end were astonished as she chanted prayers throughout the night into the morning and recited Tablets until finally her spirit was released and she yielded her last breath.

Fá'izih Khánum, age 24, in 1879

Fá'izih Khánum with her husband Áqá Siyyid Ṣádiq
and two of their adopted sons

187

Fá'izih Khánum some time after the assault by the mob, the
severe blows to her body and the loss of her right eye.

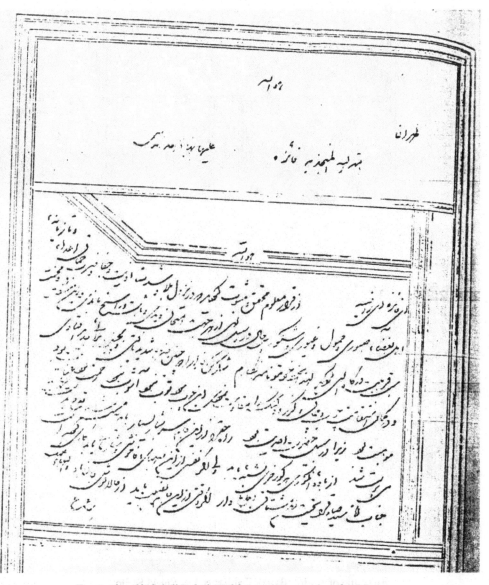

Facsimile of 'Abdu'l-Bahá's Tablet, in His own handwriting,
addressed to Fá'izih Khánum after the mob incident

189

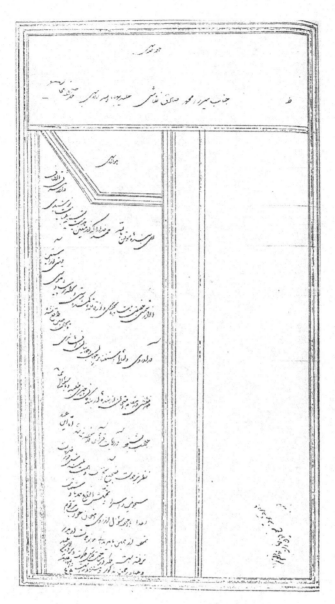

Facsimile of Abdu'l-Bahá's Tablet to Áqá Siyyid Ṣádiq
after he had received from Him the answers to all his secret
questions and had become a believer

190

NOTES & REFERENCES

1. In 1925 when Reza Shah Pahlavi seized the throne, his extreme nationalistic views brought about many changes in the country one of which was to officially replace the name "Persia", to the Western World a storied name of legend, history, poetry and song, with "Írán".

2 A pipe for smoking tobacco through water.

3. Mírzá Yaḥyá, some fourteen years younger than Bahá'u'lláh, was His paternal half-brother. Bahá'u'lláh had reared and watched over him, paying special attention to his education. The younger half-brother was thirteen years old when the Báb declared His Mission in 1844. After Bahá'u'lláh had embraced the Báb's message He helped Mírzá Yaḥyá to recognize the Báb's station and in deepening his understanding of the Writings of the Báb. At the suggestion of Bahá'u'lláh the Báb, a few months before His martyrdom, appointed Mírzá Yaḥyá nominal head of the Bábí community. Because of Bahá'u'lláh's high position and fame in the country, it was wise and necessary for His

protection that the public's attention not be drawn towards His person. Mírzá Yaḥyá's position as nominal leader enabled Bahá'u'lláh to guide the Bábí community and direct affairs from behind the scenes until it was time for Him to reveal His station.

In His Book the Bayán and in many of His other Writings, the Báb had established a firm and irrevocable Covenant with His followers concerning the Revelation of "Him whom God Shall Make Manifest", One who was the source of His own Revelation, the Object of His adoration and for Whom He longed to lay down His life. He therefore did not appoint a successor to Himself. Yet Mírzá Yaḥyá, later on, broke the Báb's Covenant when he declared himself the Báb's successor. He failed, however, to find much support for his claim among the Bábís, who almost universally accepted Bahá'u'lláh as the One whose advent was promised by their martyred Prophet.

Mírzá Yaḥyá was a cowardly yet ambitious man, easily influenced by people. He followed Bahá'u'lláh in His exiles to Baghdád, Iráq and later to Constantinople and Adrianople in Turkey, but always in the garb of disguise for fear of being recognized by the authorities. With the help of a close associate, a certain Siyyid Muḥammad-i-Iṣfahání (known as the Anti-Christ of the Bahá'í Revelation) he used every means to rebel against Bahá'u'lláh and stir up dissention among His followers; save for a small number, they all rejected him. Finally he turned to the authorities of the Ottoman Empire to arouse their wrath by bringing false charges and accusations against Bahá'u'lláh. His efforts succeeded in inflicting on Bahá'u'lláh yet another exile resulting in His imprisonment in the fortress of the penal colony of 'Akká, Palestine. Mírzá Yaḥyá was banished to the Island of Cyprus where, crushed and forlorn, he died in 1912.

4. Qur'án 9:28

5. Bahá'u'lláh Gleanings, 95:6

6. The Kitáb-i-Íqán (Book of Certitude) was revealed by Bahá'u'lláh in Baghdád about two years before His Declaration. It was written within two days and two nights in honour of Ḥájí Mírzá Siyyid Muḥammad, the oldest of the three uncles of the Báb. He did not recognize his nephew's station and claim until he met Bahá'u'lláh in Baghdád and, in answer to his questions, received the Kitáb-i-Íqán. Reading it dispelled all his doubts and enabled him to reach the stage of certitude.

Shoghi Effendi, the Guardian of the Bahá'í Faith, in his book, 'God Passes By', describes the Kitáb-i-Íqán in these words: "Foremost among the priceless treasures cast forth from the billowing ocean of Bahá'u'lláh's Revelation ranks the Kitáb-i-Íqán (Book of Certitude)...A model of Persian prose, of a style at once original, chaste and vigorous, and remarkably lucid, both cogent in argument and matchless in its irresistible eloquence, this book, setting forth in outline the Grand Redemptive Scheme of God, occupies a position unequalled by any work in the entire range of Bahá'í literature except the Kitáb-i-Aqdas, Bahá'u'lláh's Most Holy Book."

7. One of the distinguishing features of the Bahá'í Faith is the Founder's appointment of a successor in His Will and Testament. In it Bahá'u'lláh has explicitly directed His followers to turn to His eldest son, 'Abdu'l-Bahá, as the sole interpreter of His Words, expounder of His Teachings and the Centre of His Covenant. Never before in the history of Religion had it's Founder left behind an authoritative statement designating a successor to Himself and establishing a firm and indisputable Covenant with His people. Otherwise the unity of the Cause, a distinguishing feature and pivotal point of Bahá'u'lláh's Teachings, would have been destroyed by the rise of many schisms, as has taken place in earlier Religions. Nevertheless there were some egoistic and envious indviduals with a lust for power who, while claiming to be believers, opposed the Centre of the Covenant, 'Abdu'l-Bahá, and did everything in their power to disrupt the foundation of the Covenant of Bahá'u'lláh. These unfaithful, spiritually blind and lifeless individuals, included among them 'Abdu'l-Bahá's younger half brother, Mírzá

Muḥammad-'Alí, are referred to in the Bahá'í
Faith as 'violators of the Covenant' or
'Covenant-breakers'. To protect the Cause from
the poison of Covenant-breaking, such violators,
however few, have been, and will continue to
be, expelled from the Bahá'í community.

8. Ḥájí Mírzá Ḥaydar-'Alí, a native of Iṣfahán, was
a renowned Bahá'í teacher and an early disciple
of Bahá'u'lláh. He dedicated his whole life to
the service of the Faith and suffered much persecution and many years of imprisonment in
Persia, Egypt and Sudan because he persisted
audaciously in teaching the Faith. His loyalty to
the Covenant was unswerving and he served
both Bahá'u'lláh and 'Abdu'l-Bahá with great
devotion, humility and staunchness. He has also
authored several treatises and a book about his
long and remarkable life entitled Biḥjatu's-
Sudúr. A brief translation of this book into
English by Hand of the Cause of God Abú'l-
Qásim Faizí is called, 'Stories from the Delight
of Hearts'. He traveled to the Holy Land on
several occasions and attained the presence of
both Bahá'u'lláh and Abdu'l-Bahá, each time
remaining several months before being instructed to leave, on special assignments, to various
parts of the world. He spent the last years of his
life in the Holy Land where he passed away on
August 27, 1920 and was buried on Mount
Carmel.

9. Bahá'u'lláh, towards the end of His earthly life, appointed four of His most loyal, devoted and learned followers as the Hands of the Cause of God and in many Tablets revealed in their honour He referred to them as, 'the chosen ones', 'the detached souls', 'the loved ones', 'the pure in spirit'. 'Abdu'l-Bahá has defined the duties of the Hands of the Cause in the following passage from His Will and Testament: "The obligations of the Hands of the Cause of God are to diffuse the Divine Fragrances, to edify the souls of men, to promote learning, to improve the character of all men and to be, at all times and under all conditions, sanctified and detached from earthly things. They must manifest the fear of God by their conduct, their manners, their deeds and their words".

Certain outstanding believers were named post-humously by Abdu'l-Bahá as Hands of the Cause during His ministry as did the Guardian Shoghi Effendi when he designated ten such loyal and self-sacrificing souls posthumously to the same rank. It was not until 1951 that the Guardian appointed the first contingent of twelve Hands of the Cause followed, gradually, by further appointments, until one month before his death in November 1957. At that time five Hands had passed away leaving a total of twenty-seven. At the present time, 46 years later, only one beloved Hand is still in our midst, Jináb-i-Dr.'Alí-Muḥammad Varqá, who is also the Trustee of Ḥuquq'ulláh (the Right of God).

10. The Caliphate came into being within Islám after the death of the Prophet Muḥammad. Since Muḥammad's appointment of His successor, His cousin and son-in-law, Imám 'Alí, was made verbally to a large number of His followers at Ghadir-i-Khumm, it was not considered binding by the majority of the Muslims headed by Umar. Although Umar was considered one of the Prophet's stanch disciples, he broke the unwritten Covenant of Muḥammad, usurped 'Alí's right of succession and decided that successorship should be an elective process. He rallied the people around Abu-Bakr, the Prophet's father-in-law, who became the first Caliph. An old man, Abu-Bakr died two years later and was replaced by Umar who became the second Caliph of Islám. As a result of Umar's disobedience, the Muslims almost immediately became divided into two major sects, the Sunnís who followed the Caliphs and the Shí'ahs who believe in the lawful succession of the Imáms and that they were endowed with Divine guidance.

11. Qur'án, 2:207

12. Gleanings, no. CX1V.pp. 234-35

13. Ibid, no. C.p. 202

14. God Passes By, p. 299

15. Qur'án, 2:150

16. Kitáb-i-Aqdas, p.185, n.40

17. Gleanings, no. XL111, p. 93

18. Qur'án, 15:11

19. Qur'án, 34:43

20. ibid

21. ibid

22. Qur'án, 16:43

23. Qur'án, 36:60

24. Qur'án, 18:6

25. Qur'án, 3:184

26. Furúghíyyih Arbáb, "Akhtarán-i-Tábán" BE.126, pp. 275-285 and Star of the West, March 2, 1915 issue, (Persion section)

27. Qur'án, 8:31

Houri Faláhi-Skuce is the grand daughter of Jináb-i-Fádil-i-Shírází and was born in Tihrán, Írán. In her early teens she left Írán to attend boarding school in England. After graduating from high school she pioneered with her family to Lausanne, Switzerland in 1956, where she earned a diploma in several branches of medical laboratory technology while also serving on the Local Spiritual Assembly. Her work later took her to Basel where she served on the Spiritual Assembly with famed painter, Mark Tobey. In 1967 she pioneered to Canada to help form the first Spiritual Assembly in the area of North Bay, Ontario. Having married William Skuce, a Canadian artist, the couple, at the request of the National Spiritual Assembly, moved to Canada's Northwest Territories where they served three years as directors of Bahá'í House, Yellowknife. Pioneering then, to Fort Smith, NWT, they helped form its first Spiritual Assembly in 1971. By 1974 they had left the North and were homefront pioneering in Colwood, British Columbia, helping to form the first Spiritual Assembly there. In 1980 Houri, with her husband and their daughter Anisa, pioneered to Costa Rica, Central America where, during her eighteen years in that country, she served on Local Assemblies, the National Spiritual Assembly and enjoyed the bounty of attending four International Bahá'í Conventions as a delegate from Costa Rica. Moving back to Canada's West Coast in 1998, she was appointed by the National Spiritual Assembly to serve on the School Committee of Maxwell International Bahá'í School in Shawnigan Lake, British Columbia, a community where, until the time of publication, she has served on its Local Spiritual Assembly.

Printed in the United States
By Bookmasters